Order this book online at www.trafford.com
or email orders@trafford.com

Most Trafford titles are also available at major online book retailers.

Photographs by Antonio Bruzzese

© Copyright 2009 Pasquale Macrì.
All rights reserved. No part of this publication may be reproduced, stored in a retrieval system, or transmitted, in any form or by any means, electronic, mechanical, photocopying, recording, or otherwise, without the written prior permission of the author.

Print information available on the last page.

ISBN: 978-1-4251-7252-7 (sc)
ISBN: 978-1-4269-9031-1 (e)

Because of the dynamic nature of the Internet, any web addresses or links contained in this book may have changed since publication and may no longer be valid. The views expressed in this work are solely those of the author and do not necessarily reflect the views of the publisher, and the publisher hereby disclaims any responsibility for them.

Any people depicted in stock imagery provided by Getty Images are models, and such images are being used for illustrative purposes only.
Certain stock imagery © Getty Images.

Trafford rev. 03/05/2019

 www.trafford.com

North America & international
toll-free: 1 888 232 4744 (USA & Canada)
fax: 812 355 4082

Chef Pasquale

Chef Pasquale is Pasquale Macrì. Pasquale Macrì was born in 1966 in southern Italy, in the province of Reggio Calabria.

In 1984, Pasquale moved to northern Italy where he started and perfected his culinary career. Then in 1992 he married an Italian-American and moved to upstate New York. In the summer of 1993, he and his wife opened a restaurant in Albany, New York. Then in the summer of 1997, Chef Pasquale moved back to northern Italy with his wife and 2 children, where they have opened their own restaurant, ½ hour outside of Milan.

Pasquale puts creativity and passion into creating his dishes. Pasquale's wife says that he can create a meal out of practically nothing. Pasquale has decided to write this cookbook, filled with simple and quick recipes because he believes that everyone should experience the joys of cooking. Chef Pasquale hopes that everyone who purchases his cookbook will enjoy cooking his dishes as much as he does.

Contents

Appetizers—Antipasti	8
Soups—Zuppe	30
Salads—Insalate	36
Pasta Dishes—Prima di Pasta	42
Beef Dishes— Secondi di Manzo	82
Veal Dishes— Secondi di Vitello	94
Pork Dishes— Secondi di Maiale	110
Chicken Dishes— Secondi di Pollo	114
Turkey Dishes— Secondi di Tacchino	122
Seafood Dishes—Secondi di Pesce	125
Vegetable Dishes—Secondi di Verdura	140
Side Dishes—Contorni	143
Desserts—Dolce	148
INDEX OF RECIPES	165

Appetizers
Antipasti

Toasted Bread with Tomatoes Bruschetta

A loaf of Italian bread
2 large tomatoes, chopped to ¼ inch pieces
1 to 3 Tbsp. olive oil
1 garlic clove, finely chopped (optional)
A pinch of black pepper
Salt as much as needed
1 Tbsp. Basil, finely chopped
½ tsp. Oregano
1 tsp. Parsley, finely chopped

Heat oven to 400°. Cut bread loaf into 8 (½ inch to ¾ inch) slices. Place bread slices on a cookie sheet; place into oven and bake until toasted one side. Turn and toast on the other side; take out of oven and set aside. Mix all the ingredients and mix well. Let the mixture sit for 30 minutes before use. Spoon tomatoes over the toasted bread. Serves 4 people.

Tomatoes and Fresh Mozzarella Caprese

4 tomatoes
4 fresh mozzarellas
4 to 8 Tbsp. olive oil
Salt (as much as needed)
1 Tbsp. Basil

Slice tomatoes and mozzarella into ½ inch pieces. Place on a platter or 4 separate dishes alternating between tomatoes and mozzarella. Sprinkle with salt. Drizzle olive oil over top. Decorate with chopped and whole basil. Serves 4 people.

Grilled Vegetables
Verdure alla Griglia

1 large eggplant
1 large zucchini
4 small tomatoes
1 sweet red pepper
1 sweet green pepper
1 sweet yellow pepper
1 large onion
1 large radicchio (red chicory)
4 Tbsp. vegetable oil
4 Tbsp. olive oil
A pinch of salt
A pinch black pepper
Parsley as much as desired.

Heat a flat grill (or a barbeque) for 15 minutes before cooking vegetables. Peel and slice the eggplant into 8 (¼ inch) pieces. Set in a large platter. Wash and slice the zucchini diagonally into 8 (½ inch) pieces. Add to the platter. Wash and slice the tomatoes into 8 (½ inch) pieces. Add to the platter. Wash and slice the red, green and yellow peppers into ¾ inch pieces. Add to the platter. Slice the onion very thinly. Add to the platter. Slice the radicchio into 8 (½ inch) pieces, leaving a piece of stem on each piece. Add to the platter. Drizzle the vegetable oil, evenly over the vegetables. Sprinkle salt and black pepper evenly over the vegetables. Place the radicchio and sweet peppers on the grill. Grill until well cooked on one side, then turn. Then add the eggplant and zucchini. Grill until well cooked on one side, then turn. Always keeping and eye on the radicchio and peppers, if cooked take off and set in a platter or separate evenly into 4 dishes. Add the tomatoes and onion. Grill until well cooked on one side, then turn. Always keeping an eye on the eggplant and zucchini, if cooked take off and add to platter or separate evenly into 4 dishes. When the tomatoes and onion are cooked take off of grill and add to platter or separate evenly into 4 dishes. Drizzle the olive oil evenly over the vegetables. Add the parsley and serve warm. Serves 4 people.

Marinated Tuna Fish
Tonno Marinato

1 lb. Tuna or Salmon, Swordfish (or a combination)
1 c. olive oil
Juice of 1 lemon
1/8 tsp. of salt
1/8 tsp. of black pepper
1/8 tsp. of oregano
1 tsp. chopped parsley
1 tsp. chopped basil
1 garlic clove, finely chopped (optional)
lemon wedges

Place all the ingredients except for the fish in a small bowl. Mix until well blended. Set aside. Slice the fish to ¼ inch thick slices or have it sliced at the fish store. Place in a deep dish.

Pour the dressing over the fish. Refrigerate for at least 3 hours before serving. Serve cold with lemon wedges. Serves 4 people.

Steamed Clams
Vongole al Vino Bianco

2 doz. clams
1 garlic clove, finely chopped
1 oz. butter
½ c. white wine
¼ c. water
1 tbsp. parsley, chopped
Lemon wedges.

Wash clams. Place oil, garlic and clams in a large frying pan, cook on high heat for 1 minute.

Add wine, water and parsley; cook on high heat until all clams are open. (if a clam does not open throw it out, do not try opening it in any way). Take out clams; flour butter and add to sauce. Cook on medium heat for 1 minute. Pour over clams and serve with lemon wedges. Serves 4 people.

Clams and Mussels in Marinara Sauce
Zuppa di Cozze e Vongole

2 doz. clams
2 doz. mussels
1 (8 oz.) can peeled tomato, crushed
2 Tbsp. olive oil
1 garlic clove, finely chopped
½ c. white wine
Pinch of salt
Pinch of black pepper
1 tsp. parsley, chopped

Wash clams well. Set aside. Pull cord on mussels (if still attached), wash well. Set aside.

In large frying pan add olive oil, black pepper, and garlic; stir fry on medium heat until lightly browned then add the clams and mussels. Cover until the clams and mussels are all opened. (if some clams and mussels do not open throw them out do not try opening them in any way). Add the white wine and cook on medium heat until wine has evaporated, approximately 2 minutes. Add the tomato and parsley. Cook on medium heat for 8 to 10 minutes. Place on serving platter or on 4 separate plates and pour the sauce over the top. Serves 4 people.

Mussels in White Wine Sauce
Cozze Marinara

2 doz. mussels
¾ c. white wine
2 Tbsp. olive oil
1 oz. butter
1 garlic clove, finely chopped
1 tbsp. parsley, chopped
1/8 tsp. black pepper
1/8 tsp. oregano
lemon wedges

Pull cord on mussels(if still attached), wash mussels well. In large frying pan, add olive oil, black pepper, oregano and garlic; stir fry on medium heat until lightly browned, then add the mussels and cover until mussels are all opened (if a mussel does not open throw it out do not try opening it in any way). Add the wine and parsley; flour the butter and add to the pan. Cook on medium heat for 5 minutes. Place on a serving platter or separate into 4 dishes and pour the sauce over them. Serve with lemon wedges. Serves 4 people.

Pasquale Macrì

Mussels in Red Sauce
Cozze Pepate

2 doz. mussels
1 (8 oz.) can crushed tomato
¾ c. white wine
3 Tbsp. olive oil
1 small onion, thinly chopped
1 garlic clove, finely chopped
1 tsp. chopped parsley
Pinch of salt
¼ tsp. black pepper
¼ tsp. oregano

Pull cord on mussels(if still attached). Wash mussels well. In large frying pan add olive oil, onion, black pepper, oregano and garlic; stir fry on medium heat until lightly browned then add the mussels and cover until mussels are all opened (if a mussel does not open throw it out do not try opening it in any way). Add the wine; cook on medium heat until the wine has evaporated then add tomato and parsley. Cook on medium heat for about 8 to 10 minutes. Place on a serving platter or separate into 4 dishes and pour the sauce over them. Serves 4 people.

Baked Clams or Mussels
Cozze o Vongole Gratinate

10 oz. breadcrumbs
Parsley (as much as desired)
Basil (as much as desired)
1 garlic clove, finely chopped
Pinch of black pepper
Lemon wedges
2 to 4 oz. white wine
2 to 4 oz. olive oil
2 doz. Clams
2 doz. mussels

Place the breadcrumbs, parsley, basil, garlic and black pepper in a large bowl. Add 2 ounces wine and 2 ounces olive oil. Stir the mixture until it is damp. The mixture has to be able to stick together; if not add the rest of the wine and oil. Set aside. Wash clams well. Place in large pan, add ½ c. of water and place on high heat until clams are all open (if a clam does not open throw it out do not try opening it any way). Place under running cold water, wash and leave on a ½ shell. Set aside. Pull cord on mussels (if still attached), wash mussels well. Place in large pan, add ½ cup of water and place on high heat until mussels are all open (if a mussel does not open throw it out do not try opening it in any way). Place under running cold water, wash and leave on a ½ shell. Set aside. Heat oven to 400°. Fill each clam and mussel with the breadcrumb mixture. Place the clams and mussels on an oven pan. Place in oven; bake until golden brown.

Serve with lemon wedges. Serves 4 people.

Baked Scallops
Capesante Gratinate

16 Scallops with shell
1 Zucchini
½ red sweet pepper
1 small carrot
1 celery slice
1 small potato
½ onion, finely chopped
1 clove of garlic, finely chopped
2 Tbsp. butter
¼ c. vegetable oil
3 Tbsp. heavy cream.
1 tsp. basil, finely chopped
1 tsp. parsley, finely chopped
¼ tsp. salt
a pinch of black pepper
enough bread crumbs to cover the scallops.
¼ c. white wine

Heat oven to 350°. Using a potato peeler. Slice all the vegetable. Place the oil and butter in a large non stick pan. When the butter is melted, add all the vegetables and all seasonings. Stir fry on medium heat for 5 minutes. Add ¼ cup of water or fish broth. Cook for another 5 minutes. Add the heavy cream. Cook for another 5 minutes. Place the scallops on an oven pan. Distribute the vegetables evenly over the scallops. Cover lightly with the bread crumbs. Drizzle the white wine evenly over the bread crumbs. Place in oven. Bake until golden brown. Serves 4 people.

Clams Casino
Vongole Ripiene

2 doz. Clams
6 oz. imitation crab meat, chopped
2 oz. pancetta, chopped
3 oz. unsalted crackers
½ c. red roasted peppers
2 Tbsp. parmigian cheese
1 Tbsp. olive oil
Pinch of parsley
Pinch of black pepper
Pinch of basil
¼ c. white wine
¼ c. lemon juice
2 oz. butter

Wash and dry clams well. Place clams in a large frying pan. Add ½ cup water. Cook on high heat until clams are all open (if a clam does not open throw it out do not try opening it in any way). Take clams out of pan and run under cold water. Save juice in frying pan for later use. Leave the clams on a half shell. Using the same pan, place the olive oil in the frying pan. Add all ingredients except for crackers and parmigian cheese. Stir fry for 2 minutes or until the ingredients become soft. Place all the ingredients plus 2 tablespoons of the juice left over from the clams in a food processor. Process until stuffing is formed. Try forming a small ball with the stuffing if the ball forms the stuffing is ready if not add some more juice. Place stuffing on each clam until well covered. Heat oven to 400°. Place clams in an oven proof pan. Pour the wine and lemon juice in the pan not over the clams. Flour the butter and add to the wine and lemon.

Place in oven and cook until golden brown. Place on serving platter and pour the juice in the pan over the clams. Serve with lemon wedges. Serves 4 people.

Fried Squid or Fried Mixture
Calamari Fritti o Fritto Misto

2 lbs. calamari, cleaned, wash and cut into ¾ inch rings
2 doz. Shrimp (optional)
2 doz. Sardines (optional)
Enough vegetable oil to fry seafood
Enough flour to flour seafood
Lemon wedges
Salt

Drain squid well until dry; if needed dry with paper towels. Flour calamari, shrimp and sardines; shake off excess flour. Place vegetable oil in a deep frying pan. Heat oil until it bubbles. Fry squid until they come to top of oil and they are golden brown. Take out of pan and put on a paper towel to drain off excess oil. Place in dishes and sprinkle with salt to your liking.

Serve with lemon wedges. Serves 4 people.

Squid and Artichoke Salad
Insalata di Calamari e Carciofi

1 lb. calamari, cleaned,
4 Fresh Artichokes Hearts
1 doz. Shrimp
8 Asparagus Spears, boiled, cut into 1 inch diagonal pieces
8 cherry tomatoes, cut into fourths
½ cup olive oil
1 oz. butter
½ onion, finely chopped (optional)
1 garlic clove, finely chopped
1¼ Tbsp. salt
pinch of black pepper
½ tsp. parsley, finely chopped
1 Tbsp. Basil, finely chopped
1 Lemon

Cut the artichoke hearts in half. Take out any fussy part. Place in water. Squeeze ½ a lemon in the water. Set aside. Fill up half way a medium sized pan with water. Add 1 tablespoon of salt. Bring to a boil. Add the calamari. Bring to a boil and cook for 20 minutes. Drain and set aside to cool off. Place in a non stick frying pan ¼ cup olive oil, butter, onion, garlic, asparagus, shrimp, tomatoes, a pinch of salt, a pinch of black pepper, ¼ teaspoon parsley, a ¼ teaspoon basil and ½ teaspoon of lemon juice. Sauté for 5 minutes. In the meantime, cut the calamari into small rings. Place in a large bowl. Drain the artichoke hearts. Add to the calamari. Season with the remaining ingredients. When ready add the sautéed ingredients. Serves 4 people.

Seafood Salad, Marinated Octopus & Octopus Salad

Octopus Salad
Insalata di Piovra

2 medium sized octopus
½ c. olive oil (more if desired)
Juice of 1 lemon
salt (as much as needed)
Pinch of black pepper
1 tsp. Parsley, chopped
1 Tbsp. basil, chopped

Boil octopus until you can pass a fork through without problems, but do not overcook. Run under cold water until the octopus is cold. Always under running water, clean it by taking all the purple skin off the bottom of the octopus. Chop diagonally into ½ inch to 1 inch pieces. Add all the other ingredients and stir well. Refrigerate for at least 1 hour before serving. Serve cold with lemon wedges.

Variation: This dish can be made to be served warm.
Additional ingredient: 4 small boiled potatoes, cut into 1 inch cubes.

Follow the recipe as above. Add the potatoes. Place all ingredients in a medium sized, non stick frying pan. Sauté over low heat for approximately 5 minutes. Serve Warm. Serves 4 people.

Marinated Octopus
Tagliata di Piovra

2 medium octopus
½ c. olive oil
Juice of 2 lemons
salt (as much as needed)
Pinch of black pepper
1 tsp. parsley, finely chopped
1 Tbsp. basil, finely chopped
1 Tsp. oregano
¼ tsp. salt, more if desired.
20 cherry tomatoes, cut in fourths
2 bunches of Arucola, washed and chopped

Boil octopus until you can pass a fork through without problems, but do not overcook. Take out of water. (save ½ cup of the water). Let the octopus cool off for about 30 minutes. Under cold running water, clean the octopus by taking all the purple skin off the bottom of the octopus. Place the octopus in a container large enough to fit. Use any shape you like. Preferably round. Add the water that you saved before. Place something heavy over the container with the octopus. Leave at room temperature for 24 hours. Then place in the refrigerator, always with the weight on top for another 24 hours. When ready to serve, slice very thinly. (If available use a slicing machine). Place on serving platter. Add ¼ cup of olive oil and lemon juice. Set aside for 30 minutes. Place in a large bowl the tomatoes and arucola with remaining oil and all the other seasonings. Mix well. Place over the octopus. Serve cold with lemon wedges. Serves 4 people.

Pasquale Macrì

Seafood Salad
Insalata di Mare

2 doz. clams
2 doz. mussels
2 doz. large shrimps
1 doz. cleaned calamari
½ c. giardiniera
1 romaine lettuce (optional)
½ c. olive oil
The juice of 2 lemons (more or less as desired)
1 tsp. parsley, chopped
1 Tbsp. basil, chopped
salt (as much as needed, depends on the fish)
A pinch of black pepper
Lemon wedges

Wash clams; place them in large frying pan. Add ½ cup water and cook on high heat until all clams are opened, (if a clam does not open throw it out, do not try opening it); run under cold water until cold. Take clams out of shell and place in large bowl. Pull cord off of mussels (if still attached) and wash mussels well; place them in large frying pan. Add ½ cup water and cook on high heat until all mussels are opened (if a mussel does not open throw it out, do not try opening it). Run under cold water until cold. Take mussels out of shell and add to clams. Clean shrimps; boil for 3 minutes in about 6 cups water. Run under cold water until cold and add to bowl. Wash calamari and boil on medium heat for 5 minutes or until cooked (fork goes through them easily); run under cold water until cold. Cut into ½ inch rings and add to bowl. Drain and rinse the giardiniera; cut the giardiniera into small pieces if big. Add to bowl. If adding romaine lettuce, wash and drain well. Take off the outside leaves of the romaine lettuce; cut the rest of the romaine lettuce thinly and add to bowl. Season the fish salad, with the rest of the ingredients, to your liking. Refrigerate for at least 1 hour before serving. Serve cold with lemon wedges. Serves 4 people.

Shrimp and Asparagus Salad Mare e Monti

16 large shrimps
¾ c. boiled asparagus tips
6 oz. cannellini beans
Juice of one lemon
5 Tbsp. olive oil
1 Tbsp. basil, finely chopped
1 tsp. parsley, finely chopped
Salt–(as much as needed)
Lemon wedges

Clean shrimp and put in boiling water for about 2 minutes; drain. Cut shrimps in half; place in large bowl. Cut asparagus into about 1 inch pieces; add to shrimp. Wash and drain well the cannellini beans; add to shrimps and asparagus. Add all other ingredients and stir well. Refrigerate for at least 1 hour before serving. Serve cold with lemon wedges. Serves 4 people.

Shrimp and Asparagus Salad II Mare e Monti II

16 large shrimps
¾ c. boiled asparagus tips
12 Cherry tomatoes
1 tsp. chopped onion
5 Tbsp. olive oil
1 Tbsp. butter
¼ tsp. chopped garlic (optional)
½ tsp. basil, finely chopped
½ tsp. parsley, finely chopped
Salt–(as much as needed)
A drop of lemon juice

Clean shrimp and set aside. Cut asparagus into about 1 inch pieces and set aside. Cut tomatoes into 4 and set aside. Place olive oil and butter in a medium sized non stick pan and place over low heat. When the better is melted add the tomatoes and sauté on low heat for 2 minutes. Add all other ingredients, except for lemon juice. Sauté for about 4 minutes or until the shrimps are cooked (the shrimps will be rose colored). Take off of heat and stir in the lemon juice. Serve warm. Serves 4 people.

Fried Mozzarella
Mozzarella Fritta

1 lb. mozzarella (chunk)
1 to 2 lbs. breadcrumbs
4 to 6 beaten eggs
A pinch of black pepper
A few basil leaves
½ tsp. oregano
Parsley (as much as desired)
Enough flour to flour the mozzarella
Enough vegetable oil to fry the mozzarella
Marinara Sauce (optional)

Cut mozzarella into 1 inch pieces (can leave as one whole piece or make 1inch sticks). Place the beaten eggs in large bowl. Place the breadcrumbs in another large bowl and add the black pepper, oregano, basil and parsley. Flour the mozzarella pieces. Pass the mozzarella pieces through the egg and then through the bread mixture. Repeat, making sure that the mozzarella pieces are well covered with the breadcrumbs, because if there is even a small piece of mozzarella showing the mozzarella will drip when fried. Place the oil in a deep frying pan, heat oil on high heat until it starts bubbling. Place the mozzarella into the oil and fry until golden brown on both sides. When cooked take out and place on a paper towel to drain the oil. Serve alone or with marinara sauce. (Recipe given in the pasta section) Serves 4 people.

Chef Pasquale's Italian Recipes

Mozzarella in a Carriage
Mozzarella in Carrozza

FOR SAUCE

1 tsp. cappers, finely chopped
4 anchovies, finely chopped
¼ white wine
¼ c. broth
1 oz. butter

Place cappers and anchovies in a small frying pan. Add white wine and cook on medium heat until wine is almost evaporated. Add broth and cook on medium heat for 1 minute. Add floured butter and cook on medium heat until creamy. Place in 4 small bowls and set aside.

FOR MOZZARELLA

8 slices white bread
1 lb. mozzarella (chunk)
1 to 2 lb. bread crumbs
5 to 8 beaten eggs
A pinch of salt
A pinch of black pepper
A few basil leaves
½ tsp. oregano
½ tsp. parsley
Enough flour to flour the mozzarella and bread squares
Enough vegetable oil to fry the mozzarella and bread squares
Marinara Sauce (optional)

Take the crusts off of the bread slices. Cut mozzarella into 4 (1inch thick) square pieces, but the width has to be as wide as the bread slice. Place the beaten eggs in large bowl. Place the bread crumbs in a separate large bowl and add the black pepper, oregano, basil and parsley. Place each mozzarella piece between two bread slices. Flour the mozzarella and bread squares. Pass the mozzarella and bread squares through the egg and then through the bread mixture. Repeat, making sure that the mozzarella and bread squares are well covered with the breadcrumbs because if there is even a small piece of mozzarella showing the mozzarella will drip when fried. Place the oil in a deep frying pan; heat oil on high heat until it starts bubbling. Place the mozzarella and bread squares into the oil and fry until golden brown on all sides. When cooked take out and place on a paper towel to drain the oil. Serve with sauce on side. (Recipe in pasta section). Serves 4 people.

Pasquale Macrì

Rolled Eggplants
Involtini di Melanzane

FOR SAUCE

1 16 oz. can peeled tomatoes-crushed
1 tsp. olive oil
1 garlic clove-finely chopped.
1 small onion – thinly chopped
½ tsp. salt
A pinch of black pepper
½ tsp. parsley
1 tbsp. basil
1 oz. butter

FOR EGGPLANT

2 large eggplant
12 slices ham
12 slices mozzarella
4 eggs
A pinch of salt
A pinch of black pepper
12 tsp. grated cheese
Enough flour to flour eggplant slices
Enough vegetable oil to fry eggplant slices

Put onion, salt, olive oil, parsley, oregano and black pepper in frying pan. Stir fry on low heat until light brown, than add tomato and butter; cook on medium heat for 15 minutes. Set aside. Peel and slice eggplant into 24 (¼" thick) slices. Pass each slice through the flour and set aside. Beat eggs; add salt and pepper. Put oil in a deep frying pan; heat on high heat until oil starts to bubble. Lower the heat to medium. Pass the eggplant slices through the egg and place in the hot oil. Fry on each side until golden brown on each side. Take out of oil; place on paper towel to drain out the excess oil and to cool off completely. Cut ham and mozzarella in half. Place a piece of ham, mozzarella and ½ teaspoon grated cheese in each slice of eggplant and roll inward until closed. Heat oven to 350°. Cover bottom of an oven proof dish with the a thin layer of tomato sauce. Place eggplant pieces over the tomato sauce, then put a spoonful of tomato sauce over the eggplant pieces.

Place the dish in the oven and bake for 15 minutes. Serve warm. Serves 4 people.

Boiled Eggs with Rosé Sauce
Uova con Salsa Rosa

8 boiled eggs
1 c. mayonnaise
½ c. ketchup
½ a shot of brandy
8 drops of Worcestershire sauce

Place eggs in a medium sized pan and cover with water. Bring to a boil over medium heat. Once the water boils cook for 10 minutes. Take eggs out of water and let them cool completely. Place all the ingredients, except for the eggs, in a medium sized bowl. Mix until well blended. Set aside. Peel and cut the eggs in half. Place in a deep dish. Cover completely with the rosé sauce.

Refrigerate for at least 3 hours before serving. Serve cold. Serves 4 people.

Omelet
Frittata

8 medium eggs
¼ c. grated cheese
1/8 tsp. salt
Pinch of black pepper
Parsley (as much as desired)
1oz. butter

OPTIONAL

Spinach, chopped
Sweet peppers, diced
Onion, chopped
Or any other vegetable desired, diced or chopped.

Beat eggs and add all ingredients. Melt butter in a medium sized, non stick frying pan. Add the egg mixture to the pan; cook covered on low heat until the edges of the egg mixture become golden brown. Take frying pan over to sink and turn the omelet onto the frying pan cover, then slide back into the frying pan. Let cook on low heat for 5 minutes or until eggs are completely cooked. Then slide onto a flat dish and cut into triangles. Serves 4 people.

soups

Soups
Zuppe

Pasta and Beans
Pasta e Fagioli

6 oz. ditalini Pasta
16 oz. cannellini beans
3 oz. pancetta (Italian Bacon), thinly chopped
2 c. peeled tomato, blended in blender
1 oz. onion, finely chopped
2 garlic cloves – finely chopped
2 Tbsp. olive oil
1 oz. butter
4 Tbsp. grated parmigian cheese
½ c. broth
A pinch of black pepper
½ tsp. basil, chopped
¼ tsp. parsley, chopped

Place the olive oil, onion, garlic and pancetta in a 2 liter pan. Stir fry on medium heat until golden brown. Add the tomato and broth; cook on medium heat for 15 minutes. Add beans, parsley, basil and black pepper; cook on medium heat for 5 minutes. Turn off heat and Set aside.

Cook the pasta according to the package (cook for 2 minutes less than the package says). Drain and add to the soup. Cook on low heat for 2 minutes. Spoon into soup bowls. Top with grated cheese. Serves 4 people.

Pasquale Macrì

Vegetable Soup
Minestrone di Verdura

2 carrots, sliced ½ inch thick
2 celery stalks, sliced ¼ inch thick
2 zucchini, cut 1 inch thick
10 oz. string beans
2 small potatoes, cut 1 inch thick
1 small tomato, cut ½ inch thick
4 oz. canned cannellini beans
4 oz. canned chick peas
4 oz. fresh or frozen peas
1 small onion, finely chopped
2 Tbsp. olive oil
1 Tbsp. salt (more if necessary)
2 liters water
8 oz. ditalini pasta (optional)

Place the olive oil in a medium sized pan. Heat oil; add the salt, onion, carrots and celery. Stir fry on medium heat until golden brown. Add the zucchini, string beans, peas and potatoes. Stir fry for 2 minutes. Add the water to the pan and cook on low heat until the vegetables are cooked. Approximately 1 hour. Add the cannellini beans and chick peas. Cook for 1 more minute. Place in four soup bowls. If you want to add the pasta to the soup, cook the pasta according to the package and add to the soup before placing in soup bowls. Serves 4 people.

Tortellini Soup
Tortellini in Brodo

12 oz. tortellini
4 ½ c. chicken or veal broth
1 Tbsp. olive oil
1 oz. floured butter
2 oz. parmigian cheese
Chopped parsley for decoration
2 eggs (optional)
2 oz. parmigian cheese

Place the broth in a medium sized pan. Bring broth to a boil. Add tortellini and cook for as many minutes as it says on the package. If you add egg, beat the eggs and add 2 oz. cheese and add to the broth when tortellini are added. Add the floured butter. Cook until the butter is melted. Shut off the heat and add the olive oil. Place in four soup bowls and add the grated cheese. Add some parsley to each bowl. Serves 4 people.

Salads
Insalate

Grand Salad
Insalatona

2 bunches arucola
2 large tomatoes
2 large fresh mozzarella
1 (16 oz.) can corn
1 romaine lettuce
2 (8oz.) cans tuna fish (in water)
4 Boiled eggs
½ c. white vinegar
½ c. extra virgin olive oil
Salt as much as desired
Pinch of black pepper

Wash and drain well the arucola and romaine lettuce. Cut and place in a large bowl. Cut the tomatoes and fresh mozzarella into ½ inch slices and add to the bowl. Wash and drain the corn, add to the bowl. Drain the tuna fish and add to the bowl. Add the vinegar, oil, salt and black pepper or use your favorite Italian dressing. Toss lightly. Cut the eggs into ½ inch slices and add to the bowl. Serves 4 people.

Chef's Salad
Insalata dello Chef

1 large romaine Lettuce
4 chicken breasts
1 lb. Pancetta (Italian Bacon)
½ c. white vinegar
8 Tbsp. extra virgin olive oil
Salt as much as desired
Pinch of black pepper

Wash the romaine lettuce and drain well. Cut romaine lettuce and place in a large bowl. Set aside. Heat the grill (or barbeque) to 400° for 15 minutes. Drizzle the vegetable oil over the chicken breasts and place on the grill. Cook for about 5 minutes on both sides or until the chicken is cooked. Set aside to cool. Cut the chicken into 1 inch pieces and add to the lettuce. Slice the pancetta into 1 inch chunks. Place the pancetta on the grill and cook for about 2 minutes on each side. Cut the pancetta into ½ inch pieces and add to the lettuce and chicken. Add all the other ingredients and stir well until well mixed. Serve immediately. Serves 4 people.

Chick Pea Salad
Insalata di Ceci

4 large tomatoes
4 large boiled potatoes
1 (16 oz.) can chick peas, washed and drained
8 Tbsp. extra virgin olive oil
Salt as much as desired
Pinch of black pepper
1 tsp. oregano
1 to 2 tbsp. basil

Cut the tomatoes and potatoes into ½ inch slices and place in a large bowl. Add all the other ingredients to the bowl. Stir until well mixed. Serve immediately. Serves 4 people.

Tomato and Red Onion Salad
Insalata Calabrese

4 large tomatoes, cut into ¾ inch pieces
1 large red onion, thinly sliced
8 Tbsp. extra virgin olive oil
salt (as much as desired)
2 Tbsp. fresh basil
½ tsp. oregano

Place all the ingredients in large bowl; stir well. Refrigerate for ½ hour and serve cold. Serves 4 people.

Summer Salad
Insalata d'estate

1 large yellow melon
4 bunches of arucola
8 hearts of palm sticks
8 Tbsp. extra virgin olive oil
Salt (as much as desired)
A pinch of black pepper

Wash and chop the arucola. Set the arucola aside to dry completely. Peel and cut melon into 1 inch cubes. Place in a large bowl. Cut the heart of palms into 1 inch thick diagonal pieces. Add to the melon. Add the arucola, olive oil, salt and pepper to the bowl. Mix well and serve immediately. Serves 4 people.

Pasta Dishes
Prima di Pasta

Pasta Salad
Penne Caprese

14 oz. Penne
2 medium tomatoes
2 fresh mozzarellas
8 Tbsp. olive oil
A pinch of black pepper
Salt
1 tsp. parsley
1 tsp. basil

Cook pasta according to package; drain. Add 2 tablespoon olive oil. Set aside to cool off completely. Chop the tomatoes and mozzarella into ½ inch pieces. Add to cold pasta. Add the remaining oil, parsley, basil, salt and black pepper. Refrigerate for 30 minutes before serving. Serves 4 people.

Pasta Salad II
Penne al Carpaccio

14 oz. Penne
½ lb. chunk of beef
2 bunches of arugola
20 cherry tomatoes
4 oz. piece Grana or Parmigian cheese
Juice of 1 lemon
8 Tbsp. olive oil
½ tsp. salt
1 tsp. basil

Wrap beef chunk in tin foil. Freeze the chunk of beef for at least a few hours. When frozen, slice the meat very thinly, if possible use a slicing machine. Set aside to defrost. Cook pasta according to package; drain and set aside to cool. Shave the cheese, with a potato peeler. Set aside. Wash and chop the arugola. Set aside to drain and dry. Cut the cherry tomatoes into 4 pieces and place in a large bowl. Add the beef slices, arucola, lemon juice, olive oil, salt and basil to the tomatoes. Let stand for 10 minutes. Add the pasta and mix well with all the ingredients. When ready to serve place the cheese shavings over the top. Refrigerate for at least 30 minutes before serving. Serves 4 people.

Pasquale Macrì

Rice Salad
Insalata di Riso

8 oz. rice
1 (8 oz.) can corn
1 (8 oz.) can peas
1 c. giardiniera, cut into small pieces
1 (8 oz.) can sweet peppers
4 to 8 oz. tuna, drained
1 large tomato, cubed to ½ inch pieces
1 fresh mozzarella, cubed to ½ inch pieces
¼ lb. ham chunk, cubed to ½ inch pieces
1/3 c. olive oil
Salt
A pinch of black pepper
¼ tsp. oregano
½ tsp. parsley
1 tsp. basil

Cook rice according to package; run under cold water for about 2 minutes. Drain and set in a large bowl. Rinse and drain well the corn, peas, giardiniera and sweet peppers. Add to the rice.

Add all the other ingredients to the rice. Season with salt, black pepper, oregano, basil and parsley. Refrigerate for at least 30 minutes before serving. Serves 4 people.

Rice with Treviso Salad and Smoked Cheese Risotto alla Trevisana

12 oz. rice
1 large treviso salad, chopped
3 Tbsp. olive oil
1 Tbsp. vegetable oil
1/8 c. white wine
1 small onion, finely chopped
A pinch of salt
A pinch of black pepper
1/8 c. red wine
1 to 3 c. broth
1 oz. butter
¼ lb. smoked cheese, chopped

Place the olive oil, vegetable oil and onion in frying pan; stir fry until golden brown. Add the rice; keep stirring the rice until well toasted. Add the white wine and cook for another 2 minutes, stirring constantly. Add the salt, pepper and the treviso salad; cook on medium heat for 2 minutes. Add the red wine and cook until the wine evaporates. Add 2 cups of broth. Stirring constantly add small amounts of broth, as needed until the rice is cooked. Approximately 15 minutes. The rice needs to be creamy not watery so be careful not to add too much broth. Add the butter and smoked cheese; stir over medium heat until they are melted. Serve immediately. Serves 4 people.

Tortellini with Ham and Cream
Tortellini Panna e Prosciutto

14 oz tortellini
1 oz. butter
10 oz. heavy cream
¼ lb. ham
1c. peas
¼ tsp. salt
Parsley enough for decoration
1 Tbsp. grated parmigian cheese

Melt butter in pan; add, salt, ham and peas. Stir fry on medium heat for 4 minutes or until golden brown. Add heavy cream and cook on medium heat until it becomes creamy. Cook Pasta according to package, drain and place in pan. Add parsley and cheese; then toss until well coated with sauce; cook for an additional minute. Serves 4 people.

Gnocchi with Eggplant and Mozzarella
Gnocchi alla Sorrentina

1 lb. gnocchi
1 medium eggplant, peeled and thinly sliced
1 lb. can peeled tomato, blended
2 Tbsp. olive oil
1 small onion, thinly sliced
1 garlic clove, thinly chopped
1 tsp. salt
A pinch of black pepper
1 c. mozzarella, chopped
4 Tbsp. grated cheese
1 oz. butter
1 Tbsp. basil, chopped

Put the oil, butter, onion, garlic, salt and eggplant in pan. Stir fry on medium heat until the eggplant is golden brown. Add the tomato. Cook on medium heat for 10 to 15 minutes. If dries up add some water. Cook the gnocchi according to the package; drain. Add to the sauce; add mozzarella, basil and grated cheese. Toss until well coated with the sauce. Cook on medium heat for an additional minute or until the mozzarella is melted. Serves 4 people.

Gnocchi with Mushrooms and Walnuts
Gnocchi con Funghi e Noci

1 lb. gnocchi
1 c. mushrooms, sliced
¼ c. walnuts
10 oz. heavy cream
¼ tsp. salt
1 oz. butter

Put butter, salt, mushrooms and walnuts in a medium sized pan. Stir fry medium heat until mushrooms and walnuts are golden brown. Add the heavy cream and cook on medium heat for about 5 minutes or until creamy. Cook gnocchi according to package; drain. Add to sauce, toss until well coated with sauce. Serves 4 people.

Gnocchi with 4 Cheeses
Gnocchi ai Quattro Formaggi

1 lb. gnocchi
4 oz. gorgonzola
4 oz. pecorino cheese
4 oz. taleggio cheese or a soft melt able cheese.
10 oz. heavy cream
1 oz. butter
A pinch of salt
Parsley just for decoration
4 Tbsp. parmigian cheese

Melt butter in pan; add salt and all the cheeses, except the grated cheese. Cook on medium heat until all cheeses are almost melted; add heavy cream. Cook on medium heat for 5 to 8 minutes or until the sauce is creamy. Cook gnocchi according to package; drain. Place in pan and toss until coated with sauce. Add parsley and grated cheese and cook for an additional minute. Serves 4 people.

Pasquale Macrì

Ravioli with Shrimp
Ravioli dello Chef

40 Ravioli
2 doz. shrimps
20 cherry tomatoes, cut into fourths
1 garlic clove, finely chopped
1 small onion, finely chopped
½ tsp. salt
1 Tbsp. olive oil
¼ c. white wine
Juice of 1 lemon

Place salt, garlic, onion and olive oil in frying pan. Stir fry until golden brown. Add the shrimps; stir on medium heat for 1 minute. Add the cherry tomatoes; cook on medium heat for 1 minute.

Add the white wine and lemon juice. Cook on medium heat for 5 minutes. Flour the butter and add to the sauce. Cook on medium heat for 5 more minutes. Cook ravioli according to package; drain. Add pasta and parsley to sauce. Toss until well coated with the sauce and cook for an additional minute. Serves 4 people.

Tagliatelle with Swordfish and Asparagus
Tagliatelle Spada e Asparagi

12 oz. tagliatelle
8 oz. swordfish, cut into 2 inch pieces
40 cherry tomatoes, cut into fourths
6 asparagus spears, boiled and cut into ½ inch pieces
½ garlic clove, finely chopped
1 small onion, finely chopped
3 Tbsp. olive oil
¼ tsp. salt
¼ c. white wine

Place oil, garlic, onion, asparagus and swordfish in pan; stir fry until golden brown. Add white wine. Cook on medium heat until wine has evaporated. Add cherry tomatoes and salt. Cook on medium heat for 8-10 minutes. Cook pasta according to package; drain. Add to sauce, toss until well coated with the sauce and cook for an additional minute. Serves 4 people.

Tagliatelle with Shrimp and Asparagus
Tagliatelle Gamberi e Asparagi

12 oz. tagliatelle
2 doz. shrimp, whole
6 boiled asparagus spears, chopped to ½ inch thick
½ garlic clove, finely chopped
2 Tbsp. olive oil
1 to ½ oz. butter
½ doz. shrimp, minced
4 oz. crabmeat, minced
½ shot brandy
¼ c. white wine
¼ tsp. salt
A pinch of black pepper
½ cup fish broth
2 oz. heavy cream or 20 cherry tomatoes cut into fourths
(if cherry tomatoes are used, use ¼ c. fish broth)
1 Tbsp. basil, finely chopped
½ tsp. parsley, finely chopped

Place oil, ½ ounce. butter and garlic in pan; stir fry until golden brown. Add the whole shrimps and asparagus; stir fry on high heat for 1 minute. Add the minced shrimp, minced crabmeat, white wine and brandy; stir fry on high heat until wine and brandy have evaporated. Flour the butter and add with the salt, pepper, fish broth and heavy cream or cherry tomatoes to the other ingredients. Cook on medium heat for 5-7 minutes or until sauce is creamy, not watery. Cook pasta according to package; drain. Add to sauce; toss until well coated with the sauce and cook for an additional minute. Serves 4 people.

Tagliatelle with Porcini Mushrooms
Tagliatelle ai Porcini

12 oz. tagliatelle
4 oz. porcini mushrooms, thinly sliced
2 Tbsp. olive oil
1 garlic clove, finely chopped
¼ tsp. salt
A pinch of black pepper
1 Tbsp. basil
½ c. to 1 c. vegetable broth
1 oz. butter

Place the oil, garlic, salt, and black pepper to pan, stir fry until the garlic is golden brown. Add the porcini mushrooms and stir fry until mushrooms are soft. Add ½ cup broth, cook on medium heat for 1 minute. Flour the butter and add to the broth. If dry add more broth if not cook until the sauce is creamy. Cook the pasta according to the package, drain and add with the basil to the sauce, toss until well coated with sauce. Serves 4 people.

Tagliatelle with Sausage and Rucola
Tagliatelle Rustiche

12 oz. tagliatelle
1 lb. sausage, cut into 1 inch pieces
2 to 4 bunches arucola, chopped
6 large fresh tomatoes, chopped
2 Tbsp. olive oil
1 small onion, finely chopped
1 garlic clove, finely chopped
A pinch of salt
A pinch of black pepper

Place olive oil, onion, garlic and sausage in frying pan; stir fry until golden brown. Add salt, pepper, arucola and tomatoes; cook on medium heat for 10 minutes. If it starts to dry add a some water. Cook the pasta according to the package; drain. Add to the sauce; toss until covered well with the sauce. Cook for an additional minute. Serves 4 people.

Tagliatelle with Filet of Sole and Spinach
Tagliatelle all'Adriatica

12 oz. tagliatelle
1 lb. filet of sole, cut into 2 inch pieces
12 oz. frozen or fresh spinach
8 oz. cannellini beans, drained
1 garlic clove, finely chopped
1 to ½ oz. butter
1 Tbsp. olive oil
¼ c. white wine
½ c. to 1 c. fish broth

Place garlic, oil, and 1 ounce butter in a pan; stir fry until garlic is golden brown. If fresh spinach wash and add to pan cook until the spinach has been absorbed by the butter and oil. If frozen, defrost then add to the pan, and cook on medium heat for 2 minutes. Add the beans, the filet of sole and the white wine. Cook on medium heat for about 5 minutes or until the wine has evaporated. Add ½ cup of the broth and cook for 2 minutes. Flour the remaining butter and add to the broth to make it become creamy. If too dry add more broth. If not, cook until sauce is creamy. Cook the pasta according to the package; drain. Add to the sauce; toss until covered well with the sauce. Serves 4 people.

Fresh Pasta with Monkfish
Pasta Fresca alla Pescatrice

12 oz. fresh pasta
8 oz. monkfish, cut into 2 inch pieces
40 cherry tomatoes, cut into fourths
1 zucchini, thinly sliced
½ garlic clove, finely chopped
1 small onion, finely chopped
3 Tbsp. olive oil
¼ tsp. salt
¼ c. white wine

Place oil, garlic, onion, zucchini and monkfish in pan; stir fry until golden brown. Add white wine. Cook on medium heat until wine has evaporated. Add cherry tomatoes and salt. Cook on medium heat for 5 to 10 minutes. Cook pasta according to package; drain. Add to sauce; toss until well coated with the sauce and cook for an additional minute. Serves 4 people.

Tagliolini with Caviar and Vodka
Tagliolini alla Russa

12 oz. tagliolini
4 tsp. red caviar
1 Tbsp. black caviar
1 shot vodka
8 oz. heavy cream
2 Tbsp. cooked tomato sauce (optional)
Parsley (as much as desired)
1 oz. butter

Melt butter in frying pan. Add the red caviar. Cook on medium heat for 1 minute. Add the vodka. Cook on medium heat until vodka has evaporated. Add the parsley, heavy cream and tomato sauce. Cook on medium heat until the sauce is creamy, about 5 minutes. Cook pasta according to package; drain. Add pasta and parsley to sauce; toss until well coated with the sauce and cook for an additional minute. Place in four dishes and sprinkle each dish with the black caviar. Serves 4 people.

Fettuccini with Salmon in a Cream Sauce
Fettuccini al Salmone

14 oz. Fettuccini
½ lb. smoked salmon, chopped or thinly sliced
½ lb. fresh salmon, cut into 1 inch pieces
10 oz. heavy cream.
¼ tsp. salt
1 Tbsp. parsley
Pinch of black pepper
1 oz. butter
Grated Parmigian Cheese

Melt butter in frying pan; add fresh salmon sauté until golden brown. Add smoked salmon and cook for another minute. Add all other ingredients in pan and cook on medium heat 5 to 10 minutes or until sauce is creamy. Cook fettuccini according to package; drain. Add to pan. Add cheese and toss until covered with sauce. Cook for an additional minute. Serves 4 people.

Pasta Marinara

14 oz. of your favorite pasta
12 oz. can peeled tomatoes
1 small onion, finely chopped
1 garlic clove, finely chopped
1 tsp. salt
A pinch of black pepper
1 tsp. parsley
1 Tbsp. basil
2 Tbsp. olive oil

Crush the tomato with your hands. Set aside. Place oil, onion and garlic in pan. Stir fry until the onion is golden brown. Add all the other ingredients. Cook on medium heat for 15 minutes. If it starts to dry add some water. Cook pasta according to package; drain. Add to sauce; toss until well coated with the sauce. Cook for an additional minute. Serves 4 people.

Pasta with Tomato Sauce
Pasta al Pomodoro

14 oz. of your favorite pasta
12 oz. can peeled tomatoes, blended
1 carrot, finely chopped
1 celery stalk, finely chopped
1 tsp olive oil
1 garlic clove, finely chopped.
1 small onion, finely chopped
1 tsp. salt
½ tsp. parsley
1 Tbsp. basil
¼ tsp. oregano
Grated Parmigian Cheese
1 oz. butter

Put onion, carrots, celery, salt, olive oil, parsley, oregano and black pepper in frying pan. Stir fry on low heat until light brown than add tomato and butter cook on medium heat for 15 minutes. If it starts to dry up add some water. Cook pasta according to package; drain. Add to sauce; toss until completely coated with sauce. Top with basil and cheese. Cook for an additional minute. Serves 4 people.

Pasta in a Meat Sauce
Pasta al Ragù

14 oz. of your favorite pasta
6 oz. ground beef
6 oz. ground pork
2 large carrots
2 celery stalks
1 small onion
1 garlic clove
2 Tbsp. tomato paste
16 oz. can peeled tomato, blended
¼ cup red wine
1 ¼ tsp. salt
A pinch of black pepper
2 Tbsp. olive oil
2 bay leaves

Process carrots, celery, onion and garlic in food processor until finely chopped. Place olive oil in pan. Add processed vegetables and salt; stir fry about 1 minute. Add meat and stir fry on medium heat until browned. Add red wine. Cook on medium heat until wine has evaporated. Add the tomato paste. Mix well. Add the crushed tomatoes. Add whole bay leaves. Cook on medium heat for about 15 minutes. If it becomes dry add some water. When cooked take out bay leaves. Cook pasta according to package; drain. Add pasta to sauce; toss until well coated. Cook for an additional minute. Serves 4 people.

Pasta in a Vegetable Ragù
Pasta con Ragù di Verdure

14 oz. of your favorite pasta
2 carrots
2 celery stalks
½ garlic clove, finely chopped
1 small onion, finely chopped
1 zucchini
1 eggplant, peeled
½ green pepper
½ red pepper
2 Tbsp. olive oil
4 Tbsp. tomato paste
16 oz. can tomato, crushed
1 tsp. salt
A pinch of black pepper

Place carrots, celery, garlic, onion, zucchini, peppers and eggplant in a food processor and process on high speed for about 2 minutes. Place oil in pan and heat on medium heat for 1 minute. Add the processed vegetables. Stir fry until vegetables are golden brown. Add the salt, black pepper and the tomato paste. Cook on medium heat for 2 minutes. Add the crushed tomato. Cook on medium heat for 15 minutes. Cook the pasta according to the package; drain. Add pasta to sauce; toss until well coated with the sauce. Cook for an additional minute. Serves 4 people.

Pasquale Macrì

Pasta in a Pesto Sauce
Pasta al Pesto

14 oz. your favorite pasta
3 oz. olive oil
2 oz. parmagian cheese
1 Tbsp. pine nuts
3 bunches of basil
4 Tbsp. heavy cream
2 doz. Clams (optional)

Blend all the ingredients in the blender until smooth. If needed add more olive oil. Place the sauce in a pan. Add the heavy cream and cook on medium heat until the sauce is creamy, approximately 5 minutes. Cook pasta according to the package; drain. Add to sauce; toss until coated with sauce. If clams are added, wash, place in pan with ½ cup water. Cook on medium heat until the clams are opened. (if a clam does not open throw it out, do not try opening it in any way) Place under running water take out of shell. Add clams to sauce before adding pasta and cook on medium heat for an additional minute. Serves 4 people.

Linguine with Ricotta
Linguine Simpatia

14 oz linguine
1 small can black olives; approx. 40 olives; whole or sliced
1 lb. can peeled tomato, crushed
1 small onion, finely chopped
1 garlic clove, finely chopped
1 Tbsp olive oil
½ tsp. salt
Pinch of black pepper
¼ tsp. oregano
2 leaves basil, chopped
1 lb. Ricotta

Put in pan onion, garlic, oil, salt, and pepper; stir fry on medium heat until onion is golden brown. Add the olives, tomato, oregano, and basil; cook on medium heat 8 to 10 minutes. Cook pasta according to package; drain. Add to sauce; toss until coated with sauce. Break up the ricotta and add to pasta. Cook on medium heat for an additional minute. Serves 4 people.

Penne with Tomato and Pesto Sauce
Penne Spadellate

14 oz. Penne
Ragù (see recipe)
8 Tbsp. pesto (see recipe)
3 oz. heavy cream
4 Tbsp. grated cheese

Follow recipe for pesto. Follow recipe for Ragu except after 10 minutes add heavy cream and pesto. Cook on medium heat for another 10 minutes. Cook penne according to package; drain. Add to sauce and toss till coated with sauce. Add grated cheese and cook on high heat for an additional minute. Serves 4 people.

Pasquale Macrì

Penne with Chicken and Vegetables
Penne Colombiana

14 oz penne
4 Tbsp. olive oil.
1 small onion, finely chopped
½ tsp. salt
1 oz. butter
¼ tsp. curry powder
10 oz. heavy cream
1 c. water
1 tsp. parsley, finely chopped
A pinch of black pepper
1 large chicken breast, cut to ½ inch pieces
1 medium zucchini, thinly sliced
½ red sweet pepper, thinly sliced
½ green sweet pepper, thinly sliced
½ yellow sweet pepper, thinly sliced
1 small carrot, thinly sliced
1 stalk celery, thinly sliced
1 small potato, thinly sliced
10 cherry tomatoes – cut into fourths

The vegetables can all be thinly sliced using a potato peeler. Put olive oil in a large frying pan. Add chicken and sauté for about 2 minutes. Add the all the vegetables, except for tomatoes. Add Stir fry on medium heat until the vegetables are soft and golden brown. Add tomatoes and cook on medium heat for 2 minutes. Add all other ingredients. Cook until sauce is creamy. Cook penne according to package; drain. Add to sauce and toss till coated with sauce. Cook for an additional minute on high heat. Serves 4 people.

Penne with Hot Tomato Sauce
Penne All'Arrabbiata

14 oz Penne
12 oz. can peeled tomatoes, blended
2 garlic cloves, finely chopped
1 tsp. salt.
2 tsp. hot crushed pepper or 2 to 4 fresh hot peppers, chopped
½ to 1 tsp. parsley, finely chopped
Grated Parmigian Cheese
3 Tbsp. olive oil
1 oz. butter

Put oil and butter in frying pan. When butter is melted add garlic and pepper. Stir fry until garlic is golden brown. Add tomato, parsley and salt. Cook for 10 minutes on medium heat. Cook the penne according to the package; drain. Add penne to the sauce. Toss until the penne are completely coated with the sauce. Add the cheese and toss for an additional minute on high heat. Serves 4 people.

Roman Penne
Penne alla Romana

14 oz Penne
1 c. sliced porcini mushrooms
2 (1 inch) pieces of your favorite roast
Sauce from a roast
1 ½ oz. butter
1 Tbsp olive oil
½ to 1 c. beef broth
4 oz. heavy cream
Parsley (as much as you like), finely chopped

Make a veal roast and set aside some sauce and some pieces of the roast. Place 1 ounce butter, olive oil and the mushrooms in a pan. Cook on medium heat until the mushrooms are golden brown. Add the pieces of roast and the sauce from the roast. Cook on medium heat for 1 minute.

Add ½ cup broth, heavy cream and ½ ounce, floured butter. Cook until the sauce is creamy, not watery. Cook pasta according to the package; drain. Add to sauce and toss until coated with sauce. Cook for an additional minute. Serves 4 people.

Penne with Eggplant and Mozzarella
Penne alla Siciliana

14 oz penne
1 lb. can tomato, crushed
1 medium eggplant, peeled and thinly sliced
¼ c. pine nuts
1 c. mozzarella, cubed
1 Tbsp. olive oil
1 garlic clove, finely chopped
1 small onion, finely chopped.
1 tsp. salt
1 Tbsp. parsley, finely chopped
1 oz. butter

Put the oil, butter, onion, garlic, salt, pine nuts and eggplant in pan. Cook on medium heat until the pine nuts and eggplant is golden brown. Add the tomatoes. Cook on medium heat for 10 to 15 minutes. If dries up add some water. Cook the penne according to the package; drain. Add to the sauce. Add the mozzarella and toss until well coated with the sauce. Cook on medium heat for an additional minute or until the mozzarella is melted. Serves 4 people.

Penne with Salmon and Arugola
Penne con Salmone e Rucola

14 oz Penne
4 oz.salmon
2 oz. smoked salmon
2 bunches arugola
10 oz. heavy cream
1 Tbsp olive oil
1 oz. butter
¼ tsp. salt
A pinch of black pepper
½ tsp. parsley, finely chopped

Put all ingredients in a pan and cook on low heat for about 5 minutes. Add heavy cream, cook on medium heat until creamy. Cook pasta according to package; drain. Add to sauce and toss until completely covered with sauce. Serves 4 people.

Penne in Rosé Sauce
Penne Macrì

14 oz Penne
1 lb can peeled tomatoes, crushed
1 c. asparagus, boiled and chopped to 1 inch pieces
½ c. peas
2 c. sliced mushrooms
¼ lb. pancetta (Italian bacon)
8 oz. heavy cream
2 Tbsp olive oil.
1 small onion, finely chopped
1 garlic clove, finely chopped
Pinch of black pepper
1 tsp. salt
1 Tbsp. parsley, finely chopped
1 Tbsp. basil, finely chopped
1 oz. butter
4 Tbsp. grated cheese

Put onion, garlic, oil, pepper and pancetta in a nonstick pan. Stir fry on medium heat for 2 minutes. Add mushrooms and butter. Cook until mushrooms are soft and golden brown. Add asparagus and peas and cook for 5 minutes. Add tomatoes, parsley and basil. Cook on low heat for 5 more minutes. Add heavy cream. Cook on low heat for an additional 5 minutes. Cook penne according to package; drain. Place in pan. Add cheese and toss until completely coated with sauce. Cook for an additional minute. Serves 4 people.

Pasquale Macrì

Penne with Mushrooms
Penne alla Boscaiola

14 oz Penne
1 lb. can peeled tomato, crushed
2 c. mushrooms, thinly sliced
2 Tbsp olive oil
1 garlic clove, finely chopped
1 small onion, finely chopped
1 tsp. salt
Pinch of black pepper
1 tsp. parsley, finely chopped

Place the onion, salt, garlic, oil, and pepper in pan. Stir fry on medium heat for 1 minute. Add mushrooms and cook until mushrooms are soft. Add the tomatoes, and parsley. Cook for on low heat for 10 minutes. Cook penne according to package; drain. Place in pan. Add cheese and toss until completely coated with sauce. Cook for an additional minute. Serves 4 people.

Penne with Vegetables
Penne Ortolana

14 oz penne
2 zucchini, thinly sliced
1 sweet pepper, thinly sliced
5 tomatoes, chopped
3 Tbsp olive oil
1 small onion, finely chopped
2 garlic cloves, finely chopped
1 tsp. salt
Pinch of black pepper
1 tsp. parsley, finely chopped
1 Tbsp. basil, finely chopped
½ c. vegetable broth
1 oz. butter

Put in pan the olive oil, onion, garlic, salt, and black pepper; cook on medium heat for 1 minute. Add zucchini, pepper, tomatoes and broth. Stir fry on medium to high heat until all the vegetables are cooked (soft and golden brown). Add parsley, basil and floured butter. Cook until the butter is melted. The sauce should be creamy, if not cook for an additional minute. Cook pasta according to package; drain. Add to sauce and toss until well coated with the sauce. Cook for an additional minute. Serves 4 people.

Penne with Crab Meat
Penne alla Polpa di Granchio

14 oz. Penne
½ lb. crabmeat
1 oz. butter
1 Tbsp. olive oil
½ garlic clove, thinly chopped
½ tsp. salt
8 oz. heavy cream
4 oz. peeled tomato, crushed

Place the butter, oil, salt and garlic in a pan. Stir fry until garlic is golden brown. Add the crabmeat to the pan and stir fry until golden brown. Add the tomatoes to the crabmeat and cook on medium heat for 5 to 8 minutes. Add the heavy cream. Cook on medium heat for 5 minutes or until the sauce is creamy. Cook pasta according to the package; drain. Add to sauce and toss until coated with sauce. Cook for an additional minute. Serves 4 people.

Penne with Shrimp, Crabmeat, Arugola and Mushrooms
Penne Mare e Monti

14 oz penne
4 bunches Arugola, washed, drained and chopped
2 c. mushrooms, thinly sliced
2 doz. medium shrimps, you can add another doz. if desired
4 oz. crab meat
8 oz. heavy cream
1 Tbsp olive oil
½ garlic clove, chopped
¼ tsp. salt
A pinch of black pepper

Place the olive oil, garlic, salt, black pepper and mushrooms in a large nonstick frying pan. Stir fry on medium heat until mushrooms are golden brown. Add the shrimps and crab meat. Cook until the shrimps become rose colored. Add the arucola and cook for about 2 minutes. Add the heavy cream and cook until the sauce is creamy. Cook pasta according to package; drain. Add to sauce. toss until well coated with the sauce. Cook for an additional minute. Serves 4 people.

Bows with Zucchini and Saffron
Farfalle Zucchine e Zafferano

14oz. Bows
2 medium size zucchini, thinly sliced
A small envelope of saffron, diluted in 1/8 c. water
10 oz. heavy cream
1 Tbsp. olive oil
1 small onion, thinly chopped
1 garlic clove, thinly chopped.
½ tsp. salt
A pinch of black pepper
½ tsp. parsley, finely chopped
½ tsp. basil, finely chopped
2 Tbsp. grated cheese

Place zucchini, onion, garlic, oil, salt, black pepper in a medium sized frying pan. Stir fry until zucchini are soft and golden brown. Add saffron and cook on medium heat for 5 minute. Add the heavy cream, parsley and basil. Cook until creamy. Cook the pasta according to the package; drain. Add pasta and cheese to the sauce. Toss until well coated with sauce. Cook for an additional minute. Serves 4 people.

Bows with Gorgonzola and Arugola
Farfalle Zola e Rucola

14 oz bows
4 oz. gorgonzola (Italian blue cheese, not the dressing)
2 bunches arugola
10 oz. heavy cream
1 oz. butter
2 oz. grated cheese
1/8 tsp. salt

Cut gorgonzola into small pieces. Place the butter and gorgonzola in a medium sized, non stick frying pan. Cook on medium heat until the gorgonzola is melted. Add the arugola and cook on low heat until arugola is absorbed by the mixture. Add the heavy cream. Cook on medium heat until creamy. Cook pasta according to package; drain. Add to sauce. Add the grated cheese and toss until completely covered with sauce. Cook for an additional minute. Serves 4 people.

Pasquale Macrì

Mexican Bows
Farfalle alla Messicana

14 oz Bows
1 lb. sausage, chopped into 1 inch pieces
1 small can Mexican beans
16 oz. can peeled tomatoes, crushed
1 Tbsp olive oil
1 garlic clove, finely chopped
1 small onion, finely chopped
A pinch of salt
½ tsp. parsley, finely chopped

Place oil, garlic, onion and salt in pan. Stir fry until sausage is golden brown. Add the tomatoes. Cook on medium heat for 10 minutes. Add the beans and cook for an additional 5 minutes. Cook the pasta according to the package; drain. Add to the sauce and toss until well coated with the sauce. Cook for an additional minute. Serves 4 people.

Bows with Cherry Tomatoes
Farfalle alla Mediterranea

14 oz bows
2 tsp. cappers (more if desired)
¼ c. black olives, sliced
Anchovies (optional)
40 cherry tomatoes, cut into fourths
2 Tbsp olive oil
1 garlic clove, finely chopped
1 small onion, finely chopped
¼ tsp. salt (no salt if anchovies are added)
A pinch of black pepper
½ tsp. oregano
1 Tbsp. basil, finely chopped
1 tsp. parsley, finely chopped
1 oz. butter

Place all the ingredients, except for cherry tomatoes, in a frying pan. Cook on medium heat for 2 minute. Add cherry tomatoes. Cook on medium heat until the tomatoes are soft (approximately 10 minutes). Add some water if sauce becomes dry. Add floured butter and cook until butter is melted. Cook pasta according to package; drain. Add to sauce and toss until completely covered with sauce. Cook for on medium heat for an additional minute. Serves 4 people.

Linguine with Pancetta
Linguine alla Amatriciana

14 oz linguine
1 can peeled tomatoes, crushed
¼ lb. pancetta (Italian Bacon)
3 Tbsp. olive oil
1 medium onion, finely chopped
¼ to ½ tsp. hot pepper
1 tsp. parsley
½ c. grated pecorino cheese

Place the olive oil, onion, pancetta, and hot pepper in a large pan. Cook on medium until onion and pancetta are golden brown. Add the tomatoes and parsley. Cook on medium heat for 10 to 15 minutes. Cook pasta according to package; drain. Add pasta to the sauce. Toss until well coated with the sauce. Cook for an additional minute. Add the pecorino cheese just before placing in dishes. Serves 4 people.

Bows with Broccoli in a Rosé Sauce
Farfalle con Broccoli in Salsa Rosa

14 oz. Bows
1 doz. large shrimp, peeled, cleaned and cut in half
1 lb. broccoli, boiled, salted and divided into small pieces
¼ lb. mozzarella, cubed
1 (16 oz.) can peeled tomato, crushed
8 oz. heavy cream
2 Tbsp. olive oil
1 small onion, finely chopped
1 garlic clove, finely chopped
A pinch of black pepper
A pinch of salt

Place olive oil, onion, garlic, black pepper, salt and shrimp in a frying pan. Stir fry on medium heat until the shrimps are rose colored. Add the broccoli and stir fry for 1 minute. Add the tomatoes. Cook on medium heat for 10 minutes. Add the heavy cream; cook on medium heat for 5 more minutes or until sauce becomes creamy. Cook bows according to package; drain. Place in pan. Toss until completely coated with sauce. Cook for an additional minute. Place into baking pan. Add the mozzarella over the top. Place under the broiler or in oven until the mozzarella has melted. Divide into four dishes. Serves 4 people.

Spaghetti with Squid in a Hot Sauce
Calamari Fra Diavolo

14 oz. Spaghetti
2 lb. squid, cut into ½ inch rings
¼ c. white wine
1 lb can peeled tomatoes, crushed
1 Tbsp olive oil.
1 small onion, finely chopped
hot crushed red pepper (as much as desired)
¼ tsp. salt
1 Tbsp. parsley, finely chopped
1 Tbsp. basil, finely chopped

Place the oil, garlic, onion, hot pepper, oregano, salt and calamari in a large frying pan. Stir fry on medium heat for 5 minutes or until the calamari are golden brown. Add parsley, basil, and white wine. Cook on medium heat until wine evaporates. Add the tomatoes and cook on low heat for 10 to 15 minutes. If sauce starts to dry up add some water. Cook pasta according to package, drain. Add to sauce and toss until well coated with sauce. Cook for one an additional minute. Serves 4 people.

Linguine with Spinach and Shrimp Linguine Fantasia

16 oz. linguine
2 doz. Shrimp, cleaned
12 oz. fresh or frozen spinach
½ c. white wine
½ c. fish broth
1 garlic clove, finely chopped
1 tsp olive oil.
½ tsp. salt
Pinch of black pepper
1 oz. butter
1 Tbsp. parsley, finely chopped
1 Tbsp. basil, finely chopped

Place the garlic, ½ the butter, oil, salt, black pepper, shrimp, spinach (if frozen defrost first) in a large sized pan. Stir fry on medium heat for 1 minute then add white wine. Cook on high heat until the wine evaporates. Add the broth. Cook on medium heat for about 5 minutes. Flour the remaining butter add to the pan. Add parsley and basil and cook 2 more minutes or until sauce becomes creamy. Cook Linguine according to package; drain. Add to sauce and toss in sauce until well coated. Cook for an additional minute. Serves 4 people.

Spaghetti in a White Clam Sauce
Spaghetti alle Vongole

16oz Spaghetti
4 doz. clams, washed
½ c. white wine
¼ c. to ½ c. water
3 Tbsp. olive oil
1 garlic clove, finely chopped.
A Pinch of salt
1 Tbsp. parsley, finely chopped
1 oz. butter

Place the oil, salt and garlic in a large frying pan. Cook on medium heat for 1 minute. Add clams and white wine to pan. Cover and let cook until all the clams are open (if a clam does not open, do not try to open in any way, throw it out). Flour butter and place in pan. Add parsley. Cook until the sauce is creamy. Take clams out of pan and set aside. Cook spaghetti according to package; drain. Place in pan. Toss until coated with the sauce. Cook for an additional minute.

Place spaghetti in dishes and put clams around spaghetti. Serves 4 people.

Spaghetti in a Red Clam Sauce
Spaghetti alle Vongole – Rosse

16oz Spaghetti
4 doz. clams, washed
¼ c. white wine
1 lb. can peeled tomato, crushed
1 Tbsp. olive oil
1 garlic clove, finely chopped
1 small onion, finely chopped.
½ tsp. salt
1 Tbsp. parsley, finely chopped

Place the oil, salt, onion and garlic in a large frying pan. Cook on medium heat for 1 minute. Add clams and white wine to pan. Cover and let cook until all the clams are open (if a clam does not open, don not try to open it in any way, throw it out). Add the tomatoes and parsley. Cook on medium heat for 10 minutes. Take clams out of pan and set aside. Cook spaghetti according to package; drain. Place in pan. Toss until coated with the sauce. Cook for an additional minute. Place spaghetti in dishes and put clams around Spaghetti. Serves 4 people.

Pasquale Macrì

Linguine with Mussels
Linguine Tarantina

14 oz linguine
48 mussels
1 (16 oz.) can peeled tomatoes, crushed
½ c. white wine
3 Tbsp olive oil
2 garlic cloves, finely chopped.
½ small onion, finely chopped
¼ tsp. salt
Pinch of black pepper
1 tsp. parsley, finely chopped
½ tsp. oregano

Pull cord on mussels, if still attached, wash mussels well and set aside. Put olive oil, onion, garlic, salt, black pepper and oregano in a large frying pan. Cook on medium heat for about 1 minute. Add mussels and wine. Cook on medium heat until all the mussels have opened (If a mussel does not open, do not try opening in any way, throw it out). Add the tomatoes. Cook on medium heat for 5 to 10 minutes. Take mussels out of sauce and set aside. Cook linguine according to package; drain. Add to sauce toss until coated with sauce. Cook for an additional minute. Place in 4 large dishes. Place 12 mussels around the linguine. Serves 4 people.

Baked Spaghetti with Seafood
Spaghetti al Cartoccio

14 oz spaghetti
1 (16 oz.) can peeled tomatoes, crushed
8 oz. heavy cream
8 squid, cleaned and cut into ½ inch rings
2 doz. shrimp, peeled
2 doz. mussels
2 doz. clams
4 oz. crab meat, chopped
¼ c. white wine
2 Tbsp olive oil
1 garlic clove, finely chopped.
1 small onion, finely chopped
Pinch of black pepper
¼ tsp. salt
1 Tbsp. parsley, finely chopped
1 Tbsp. basil, finely chopped
Pizza dough (enough to place over 4 oven dishes) or just aluminum foil.

Warm oven to 360°. Pull cord on mussels, if still attached and wash well. Wash clams well. Place mussels and clams in a pan with about 1 c. water. Cook on high heat until the mussels and clams are all opened (if a clam or mussel does not open, do not try opening it in any way, throw it out). Place under cold running water. Take them out of shell and wash. Set aside. Put onion, garlic, salt, black pepper, and oil in pan. Stir fry for 1 minute. Add wine and all the fish. Cook on medium heat until golden brown (approx. 5 to 10 minutes.) Add the tomatoes. Cook on medium heat for 10 minutes. Add heavy cream. Cook on low heat for another 5 minutes. or until sauce becomes creamy. Cook spaghetti for 5minutes less than it says on the package; drain. Toss in sauce until well coated with sauce. Place spaghetti in an oven proof dish or in four separate dishes. Cover dish with pizza dough (spread thinly) or aluminum foil. Bake in oven until the pizza dough is golden brown (approximately 5 minutes). If pizza dough was used cut open the dough, carefully as not to get burned. Cut the dough into 4 pieces (or 1 if you used 4 separate dishes). Place on dishes and place the spaghetti over the dough. Serves 4 people.

Tagliatelle with Seafood
Tagliatelle allo Scoglio

14 oz. spaghetti
2 doz. clams
2 doz. mussels
2 doz. large shrimp
8 squid, cut into ½ inch rings
4 lobsters tail meat, cut into 1 inch pieces
40 cherry tomatoes, cut into fourths
½ c. white wine
3 Tbsp olive oil
1 garlic clove, finely chopped
1 small onion, finely chopped
¼ tsp. salt
¼ tsp. black pepper
½ tsp. oregano
Parsley (as much as desired), finely chopped
Basil (as much as desired), finely chopped

Wash clams well and set aside. Pull cord on mussels, if still attached, wash mussels well and set aside. Clean shrimp but leave tail on and set aside. Place the garlic, onion, salt, black pepper, oregano and oil in a large frying pan. Cook on medium heat for 1 minute. Add squid and white wine. Cook on medium heat until calamari starts browning and wine has evaporated. Add the cherry tomatoes. Cook on medium heat for 5 minutes. (If at any moment the sauce starts drying up add some water. If water is added you may need to add some more salt. Use your judgment).

Add the large shrimps and lobster meat. Cook on medium heat for another 5 minutes. Add the clams, mussels, parsley and basil. Cook until they open and then an additional 5 minutes.(Taste the fish before turning off flame because fish doesn't always cook in the amount of time indicated.) Cook the spaghetti according to the package; drain. Add to sauce and toss until well coated with sauce. Cook for an additional minute. Place spaghetti in large platters and place the seafood around the spaghetti. Serves 4 people.

Penne with Shrimp and Zucchini
Penne dello Chef

14 oz. penne
40 shrimps, cleaned and cut in half
2 medium zucchini, thinly sliced
¼ tsp. saffron, diluted in 1 oz. water
¼ tsp. salt
2 pinches black pepper
1 garlic clove, finely chopped
½ onion, finely chopped
1 oz. butter
4 oz. heavy cream
2 Tbsp. olive oil
4 Tbsp. grated parmigian cheese

Place the olive oil, garlic and onion in medium sized pan. Cook until the onion and garlic are golden brown. Add salt, pepper, zucchini and shrimps. Stir fry on medium heat for about 5 minutes Add heavy cream, saffron, and butter and cook on high for 5 minutes or until creamy. Cook penne according to package; drain. Add to the sauce and toss until coated with sauce.

Add grated cheese and cook on high for an additional minute. Serves 4 people.

Spaghetti with Olive Oil, and Hot Pepper
Spaghetti Aglio, Olio, e Peperoncino

16 oz Spaghetti
1 c. olive oil
2 garlic cloves, finely chopped
½ tsp. hot pepper (or as much as desired)
½ tsp. salt
1 tsp. parsley, finely chopped

Place the olive oil, garlic, salt, and hot pepper in a medium sized pan. Cook on medium heat for 1 minute. Cook pasta according to package; drain. Add to sauce. Toss until well coated with the sauce. Cook for an additional minute. Serves 4 people.

Spaghetti with Clams and Mussels
Spaghetti alla Levantina

14 oz. Spaghetti
2 doz. Clams
2 doz. Mussels
¼ c. white wine
A pinch of black pepper
1 Tbsp. olive oil
1 garlic clove, finely chopped
1 small onion, finely chopped
½ tsp. parsley, finely chopped
¼ tsp. saffron, diluted in 1 ounce water
¼ c. to ½ c. fish broth
1 oz. butter
A pinch of salt

Wash clams well, and place in a pan with ½ cup water. Cook on high heat until all the clams have opened (if a clam does not open do not try opening it in any way, throw it out). Take out of shell, wash and set aside. Pull cord on mussels, if still attached, wash. Place in a pan with ½ cup water. Cook on high heat until all the mussels have opened (if a mussel does not open do not try opening it in any way, throw it out). Take out of shell, wash and set aside. (If preferred the clams and mussels can be left in the shell. Must wash very well.) Place olive oil, onion, black pepper and garlic in frying pan. Stir fry until golden brown. Add the clams, mussels, salt and white wine. Cook on medium heat until the wine has evaporated. Add the saffron and cook on medium heat for about 1 minute. Add the fish broth. Flour the butter and add it to the sauce.

Cook on medium heat until sauce has thickened. Cook pasta according to package; drain. Add pasta and parsley to sauce. Toss until well coated with the sauce. Cook _rosci additional minute. Serves 4 people.

Beef Dishes
Secondi di Manzo

Sliced Beef with Lemon Carpaccio

1 lb. chunk of beef
4 bunches of arucola
20 cherry tomatoes (optional)
¼ piece of grana or parmigian cheese
Juice of 2 lemons
1 c. olive oil
Salt
A pinch of black pepper

Freeze the chunk of beef for at least a few hours. When frozen, slice the meat very thinly; if possible use a slicing machine. Place in four flat serving dishes, then set aside to defrost. Using a potato peeler shave the cheese into very thin slices. Set aside. Meanwhile, wash, chop and set aside to dry the arucola. (If cherry tomatoes are used cut into fourths, place in a bowl, and add the arucola when dry.) Add, to the bowl the lemon, olive oil, salt as much as needed and black pepper. Mix well and place over the meat; let stand for 5 minutes. When ready to serve, place the shaved cheese over the top. Serve cold. Serves 4 people.

Beef with Rosemary
Tagliata Rosmarino

2 lb. Chunk of beef
¼ c. Vegetable oil
salt
A pinch of black pepper
1 Tbsp. Rosemary
4 Tbsp. Olive oil
1 Tbsp. Parsley, finely chopped

Heat oven to 400°. Heat grill, non-stick frying pan or barbecue. Put meat on dish. Drizzle vegetable oil on all 4 sides. Sprinkle salt and a pinch of pepper on all 4 sides. Cook meat on grill, in frying pan or barbecue on all 4 sides, enough to brown on outside but leave raw in middle. When cooked, slice the meat into ½ inch thick pieces. Flatten the meat with a meat tenderizer. Oil a non-stick baking pan with olive oil and spread meat in the pan. Add a pinch of salt, pinch of black pepper and rosemary. Cook in oven for about 5 minutes or until meat is cooked to your liking. Place on serving plate. Pour excess oil over meat. Decorate with rosemary stems. Serves 4 people.

Variation: With Arugola.
Extra ingredients: 2 bunches of Arucola, washed and chopped.

Follow recipe above. Eliminate the rosemary. Place the Arucola over the meat when the meat is on the serving platter.

Beef with Mushrooms
Tagliata con Funghi

FOR MUSHROOMS

16 of your favourite Mushrooms, thinly sliced
1/8 c. Olive oil
1/8 c. Vegetable oil
1 garlic clove, finely chopped
¼ tsp. Salt
¼ tsp. Black pepper
½ tsp. Parsley, finely chopped
½ tsp. Basil, finely chopped
¼ tsp. Oregano

FOR THE MEAT

2 lb. Chunk of beef
¼ c. Vegetable oil
salt
A pinch of black pepper
1 Tbsp. Parsley, finely chopped
4 Tbsp. Olive oil

For Mushrooms

Place both oils and garlic in a non-stick frying pan. Place on medium heat and cook until the garlic is golden brown. Add all other mushroom ingredients. Stir fry on medium heat until the mushrooms are cooked (approximately 10 to 15 minutes). Set Aside.

For the Meat

Heat oven to 400°. Heat a grill, non-stick frying pan or barbecue. Put meat on dish. Drizzle vegetable oil on all 4 sides. Sprinkle salt and a pinch of pepper on all 4 sides. Cook meat on grill, in frying pan or barbecue on all 4 sides, enough to brown on outside but leave raw in middle. When cooked, slice the meat into ½ inch thick pieces. Flatten the meat with a meat tenderizer. Oil a non-stick baking pan with olive oil and spread meat in the pan. Add a pinch of salt, a pinch of black pepper and parsley. Place the mushrooms over the meat. Cook in oven for about 5 minutes or until meat is cooked to your liking. Place on serving plate. Pour excess oil over meat. Serves 4 people.

Beef with Green Peppercorns
Tagliata al Pepe Verde

2 lbs chunk of beef
2 Tbsp. mustard
1 Tbsp. Worcestershire Sauce
1 shot of brandy
½ c. Olive oil
¼ c. Vegetable oil
2 Tbsp. green peppercorns
salt
black pepper
1 tsp. parsley, finely chopped

Heat grill, non-stick frying pan or barbecue. Put meat in dish. Drizzle vegetable oil on all 4 sides. Sprinkle salt and a pinch of pepper on all 4 sides. Cook meat on grill, frying pan or barbecue on all 4 sides, enough to brown on the outside but leave raw in the middle. When cooked, slice the meat into ½ inch thick pieces. Flatten with a meat tenderizer. Using the back of a spoon spread the mustard into a large non-stick frying pan, then add the Worcestershire sauce and olive oil. Spread slices of meat into the frying pan. Add the drained peppercorns, a pinch of salt, a pinch of black pepper and parsley. Cook on high heat for 2 minutes, then add the brandy (be careful of the flame). Cook for another minute or until the brandy has evaporated. Serve immediately. Serves 4 people.

Rolled Beef
Involtini di Manzo

16 slices thin beef
16 thin slices of pancetta
16 slices mozzarella or fontina cheese
8 slices of bread (without crusts)
16 tsp. grated parmigian cheese
2 garlic cloves, finely chopped
1 small onion, finely chopped
salt
black pepper
1 (16 oz.) can peeled tomato, crushed
¼ c. white wine
½ c. vegetable oil
Enough flour to flour the beef
Broth if needed.

Cut the bread into ½ inch pieces; place in a dish and add the white wine. Set aside. Place the meat slices on a cutting board; place in each slice a pinch of salt, a pinch of black pepper, a slice of pancetta, a slice of mozzarella or fontina, and approximately 1 teaspoon of bread. Roll inward and shut with a toothpick or with string. Flour and set aside. Warm the vegetable oil in a frying pan until bubbles begin to form. Place the rolled beef in the frying pan and fry for about 1 minute on each side or until golden brown. Take out of pan and set aside. Put the a pinch of black pepper, ¼ teaspoon. Salt, garlic, onion and tomatoes in the frying pan. Cook on medium heat for 5 minutes. Add the rolled beef to the sauce. Cook on medium heat for 8 to 10 minutes or until cooked. Add a little broth at a time if needed. If sauce begins to dry off before sauce is cooked. Take beef out; place on serving dishes and pour sauce over the top. Serves 4 people.

Steak with Balsamic Vinegar Straccetto

4 Steaks
½ c. olive oil
½ c. balsamic vinegar
¾ c. beef broth
Salt
Pinch of black pepper
1 oz. butter, floured
2 bunches of arucola
¼ to ½ lb. piece of grana or parmigian cheese

Wash, dry well and chop the arucola. Set aside. Using a potato peeler, shave the cheese. Set aside. Put steaks in dish and add a pinch of salt and a pinch of pepper on both sides. Heat olive oil in frying pan.

Place steaks in frying pan and cook on both sides till brown on the outside and raw inside. Take the steaks out of the frying pan. Put the broth, vinegar and butter into the pan. Cook on medium heat until almost creamy (approximately 1 minute). Put the steaks back into the pan and cook to your liking. If well done may have to add some more broth. Place the steaks in serving dishes. Pour sauce over the steaks. Place the arucola around the steaks. Place the shaved cheese over the arucola. Serves 4 people.

Steak with Herbs
Bistecca alle Erbe

4 steaks
½ c. olive oil
salt
A pinch of black pepper
1 tsp. oregano
1 Tbsp. basil, finely chopped
1 tsp. parsley, finely chopped
1 tsp. rosemary, finely chopped
1 tsp. sage, finely chopped
4-8 scallions

Heat oil until bubbles begin to form. Add steaks and cook on medium heat on first side, until golden brown. Place all the other ingredients on the steak and turn steak over. Cook the steaks to your liking. Place the steaks on serving dishes. Cook all the herbs for one more minute and place over the steaks. Serves 4 people.

Pasquale Macrì

Steak Pizzaiola
Bistecca alla Pizzaiola

4 Steaks
1 c. olive oil
2 garlic cloves, finely chopped
1 small onion, finely chopped
1 Tbsp. capers
½ c. olives (green, black or both)
1 (16 oz.) can peeled tomato, crushed
½ c. white wine
1 to 2 anchovies
1 Tbsp. parsley, finely chopped
A pinch of black pepper
1 tsp. oregano

Heat olive oil in frying pan until bubbles begin to form. Place the steaks in the frying pan and fry, on medium heat, on one side for 2 minutes, then turn and do the same. Take out of pan; set aside. Add the garlic and onion to the oil. Stir fry until golden brown. Add the capers, olives and white wine. Cook on medium heat until the wine has evaporated. Add the tomato. Cook on medium heat for 5 minutes. Add the parsley, a pepper and oregano. Cook for 5 more minutes. Put the steaks back into the pan. Cook until the steaks are to your liking. Preferably well done. Place steaks in serving dishes and pour sauce over the top. Serves 4 people.

Steak with Vegetables
Entrecotte alla Contadina

4 steaks
1 c. olive oil
1 tsp. oregano
Salt
Pinch of black pepper
1 Tbsp. Parsley, finely chopped
2 rosemary sticks
2 garlic cloves, whole
1 large zucchini, thinly sliced
1 medium eggplant, peeled and thinly sliced
1 treviso salad, thinly sliced
½ c. beef broth (if needed)

Heat olive oil in frying pan. Place all of the ingredients, except for the steaks, in the frying pan. Cook on medium heat for about 5 to 10 minutes or until cooked (the vegetables should be soft and golden brown). Take vegetables, except rosemary and garlic, out of frying pan and set aside. Sprinkle the steaks with a pinch of salt; place in the frying pan and cook to your liking. Place the steaks in serving dishes and place the vegetables over the top. Decorate dishes with some fresh rosemary. Serves 4 people.

Filet Mignon with Porcini Mushrooms
Filetto con Porcini

4 filet mignon steaks
2 c. porcini mushrooms, sliced
1 garlic clove, finely chopped
1 c. olive oil
¼ tsp. salt
A pinch of black pepper
1 Tbsp. parsley, finely chopped
1 Tbsp. basil, finely chopped
¼ c. white wine

Place the oil in pan and heat until it starts to bubble. Sprinkle some salt over the filet steaks. Place in the hot oil and fry on both sides until medium – rare on the inside. Take out the steaks and place the garlic and mushrooms in the oil. Cook on medium heat until mushrooms are cooked (the mushrooms have to be soft and golden brown). Add the salt, pepper, parsley and basil. Cook for one more minute. Put the filet steaks back in the pan. Cook on medium heat for 1 minute. Add the wine. Cook until the wine has evaporated. Cook the filet steaks to your liking. When the filet steaks are to your liking place them in serving dishes and place the mushrooms over the top. Serves 4 people.

Filet Mignon with Green Peppercorns
Filetto al Pepe Verde

4 filet mignon steaks
1 c. olive oil
1 Tbsp. green peppercorns (in water)
1 Tbsp. mustard
A few drops of Worcestershire sauce (optional)
½ shot of brandy
10 oz. heavy cream
½ oz. butter
¼ tsp. salt
Enough flour to flour the filets

Place the olive oil in the pan. Heat until it starts to bubble. Flour the filets and place in the hot oil. Fry on all sides until medium-rare on the inside (you can cook the filet to your liking but it is best medium-rare). Get rid of the olive oil but do not clean the pan. Melt the butter in the pan. Using the back of a spoon spread the mustard on the bottom of the pan. Add the salt, peppercorns and Worcestershire sauce. Place the filets back in the pan and add the brandy. Being very careful, make the brandy flame. When the flame dies out add the cream. Cook on medium heat until the sauce is creamy, not watery. Place the filets in serving dishes. Pour the sauce over the filets. Serves 4 people.

Veal Dishes
Secondi di Vitello

Veal in a Tuna Sauce
Vitello Tonnato

1 lb. chunk of veal
1 large can of tuna in water
10 capers
4 slices of anchovies
1 small jar of mayonnaise
½ shot white wine
2 carrots, peeled
2 celery stalks

Wrap and tie the chunk of veal in a clean, thin, cotton kitchen rag. Place the veal, carrot and celery in medium sized pan. Add enough water to cover the veal. Cook on medium heat for 1 hour. Take out and set aside to cool off completely. In the meantime, place the tuna, capers and anchovies in a food processor. Process on high speed for 1 minute. Add the white wine and process on high speed for 1 more minute. Add half the mayonnaise and process on high speed until well mixed. Place the sauce in a large bowl; add the rest of the mayonnaise and mix well until the sauce is creamy. Place the sauce in the refrigerator until ready for use. When the veal is completely cooled off slice very thin. Place in 4 flat dishes until the dishes are completely covered with the veal slices. Place 2 tablespoons of the sauce over the veal slices and spread evenly over the slices. Cut the carrots and celery stalks to ½ inch pieces and place around the dish. Serve Cold. If there is any sauce left over it can be refrigerated up to one week. The sauce and the veal also make good sandwiches. Serves 4 people.

Veal with Prosciutto and Sage Saltimbocca alla Romana

16 veal scallopini
8 slices of prosciutto (Italian Ham), cut in half
16 sage leaves
½ c. white wine
½ to 1 c. veal broth
Pinch of black pepper
2 oz. butter
Enough flour to flour the veal
Enough vegetable oil to fry the veal

Place a slice of prosciutto on each slice of veal. Place a sage leaf on top of the of the prosciutto. Pound each slice of meat with a meat tenderizer so that the prosciutto and sage remain attached. (Can even attach the prosciutto and sage with a toothpick). Place the vegetable oil in a frying pan and heat until it starts to bubble. In the meantime flour the veal, shaking off any excess flour. Place the veal slices in the hot oil. Fry on each side until golden brown. Take out of oil and set aside. Get rid of the vegetable oil from the pan but do not clean the pan. Place 1 ounce of butter and veal in the pan. Cook on low heat until the butter is melted. Add the white wine. Cook on medium heat until white wine has evaporated. Add ½ cup broth and cook on medium heat for 5 minutes. If sauce begins to dry add the rest of the broth. Flour the remaining butter and add to the sauce. Cook on medium heat until the sauce is creamy, not watery. Place in serving dishes and decorate with sage. Serves 4 people.

Veal with Ham and Cheese
Vitello alla Valdostana

16 veal scallopini
8 slices of ham, cut in half
16 slices of fontina or mozzarella cheese
8 tsp. grated cheese
4 tsp. parsley, finely chopped
½ c. white wine
2 oz. butter, floured
½ to 1 c. veal broth
Pinch of black pepper
Enough flour to flour the veal
Enough vegetable oil to fry the veal

Heat oven to 350°. Place the vegetable oil in a frying pan and heat until it starts to bubble. In the meantime flour the veal, shake off excess flour. Place in hot oil. Fry on each side until golden brown. Take out of oil and set aside. Get rid of the vegetable oil from the pan but do not clean the pan. Place 1 ounce of butter. Cook on low heat until the butter is melted. Add the white wine. Cook on medium heat until white wine has evaporated. Add ½ cup of broth and cook on medium heat for 1 minute. If sauce begins to dry add the rest of the broth. Flour the remaining butter and add to the sauce. Cook on medium heat until the sauce is creamy, not watery. Place the veal in an oven pan. Place a slice of ham on each slice of veal. Place a slice of cheese over the ham. Place ½ teaspoon of grated cheese over the fontina cheese. Place a ¼ teaspoon of parley over the cheese. Pour the sauce over the veal slices. Place in oven and cook until fontina is melted and golden. (This dish can also be made using veal cutlets, then placing the ham and cheese over the top, then placing in the oven to melt the fontina cheese. This way does not need a sauce. Serve with lemon slices). Serves 4 people.

Veal with Porcini Mushrooms
Scaloppe ai Porcini

16 veal scallopini
1 c. porcini mushrooms, sliced
Enough flour to flour the veal
Enough vegetable oil to fry veal
1 garlic clove, finely chopped
1 small onion, finely chopped
1 Tbsp. olive oil
½ c. white wine
½ c. to 1 c. beef broth
1 oz. butter
1 tsp. parsley, finely chopped

Place the vegetable oil in a frying pan and heat until it starts to bubble. In the meantime flour the veal, shake off excess flour. Place in hot oil. Fry on each side until golden brown. Take out of oil and set aside. Get rid of the vegetable oil from the pan but do not clean the pan. Place the olive oil, garlic, onion, parley and mushrooms in the pan. Cook on medium heat until the mushrooms are soft and golden brown. Add the white wine. Cook on medium heat until white wine has evaporated. Add ½ cup of broth and cook on medium heat for 5 minutes. If sauce begins to dry add the rest of the broth. Flour the butter and add to the sauce. Cook on medium heat until the sauce is creamy, not watery. Serves 4 people.

Veal in a White Wine Sauce
Scaloppe al Vino Bianco

16 veal scallopini
½ c. dry white wine
2 oz. Butter
Pinch of black pepper
1 tsp. parsley, finely chopped
Enough flour to flour veal
Enough vegetable oil to fry veal
½ c. to 1 c. beef broth
2 Tbsp. capers (optional)

Place the vegetable oil in a frying pan and heat until it starts to bubble. In the meantime flour the veal, shake off the excess flour. Place in hot oil. Fry on each side until golden brown. Take out of oil and set aside. Get rid of the vegetable oil from the pan but do not clean the pan. Place 1 ounce of butter, veal and capers, if used, in the pan. Cook on low heat until the butter is melted.

Add the white wine. Cook on medium heat for 1 minute. Add ½ cup of broth and cook on medium heat for 5 minutes. If sauce begins to dry add the rest of the broth. Flour the remaining butter and add to the sauce. Cook on medium heat until the sauce is creamy, not watery. Serves 4 people.

Pasquale Macrì

Veal in a Lemon Sauce
Scaloppe al Limone

16 veal scallopini
¼ c. dry white wine
1 lemon, sliced
2 oz. butter
½ c. to 1 c. beef broth
Pinch of black pepper
Enough flour to flour veal
Enough vegetable oil to fry veal
¼ tsp. Parsley, finely chopped

Place the vegetable oil in a frying pan and heat until it starts to bubble. In the meantime, flour the veal and place in hot oil. Fry on each side until golden brown. Take out of oil and set aside. Get rid of the vegetable oil from the pan but do not clean the pan. Place 1 ounce butter and veal in the pan. Cook on low heat until the butter is melted. Put the veal back in the pan. Add the white wine. Cook on medium heat until white wine has evaporated. Squeeze a couple slices of lemon into pan and then place remaining slices of lemon back in pan. Add ½ cup broth and cook on medium heat for 5 minutes. If sauce begins to dry add the rest of the broth. Flour the remaining butter and add to the sauce. Cook on medium heat until the sauce is creamy, not watery. Add the parsley. Cook for 1 more minute. Take out lemon slices. Divide the veal in four dishes. Serves 4 people.

Veal and Asparagus
Scaloppe con Asparagi

16 veal scallopini
16 asparagus spears, cut diagonally
16 slices fontina cheese
1 oz. butter
½ c. white wine
1 Tbsp. olive oil
½ c. to 1 c. beef broth
4 to 6 Tbsp. grated cheese
Parsley for decoration
Enough flour to flour veal
Enough vegetable oil to fry veal

Heat oven to 350°. Place the vegetable oil in a frying pan (must not have a plastic handle because it will then be placed in the oven). Heat oil until it starts to bubble. In the meantime, flour the veal slices and place in hot oil. Fry on each side until golden brown. Take out of oil and set aside. Get rid of the vegetable oil from the pan but do not clean the pan. Place the olive oil, butter and asparagus in the pan. Stir fry until golden brown. Add the veal and white wine. Cook on medium heat until wine has evaporated. Add ½ cup broth and cook on medium heat for 5 minutes. If sauce begins to dry add the rest of the broth. Flour the remaining butter and add to the sauce. Cook on medium heat until the sauce is creamy, not watery. Place a slice of fontina cheese on each slice of veal. Sprinkle cheese and parsley over the veal and place in oven until the fontina cheese is melted and golden brown. Serves 4 people.

Pasquale Macrì

Veal Pasquale
Scaloppe alla Pasquale

16 veal scallopini
2 c. boiled broccoli
1 c. sun dried tomatoes
1 c. sliced mushrooms
1 doz. Shrimps
8 oz. heavy cream
½ c. to 1 c. beef broth
2 oz. Butter
1 Tbsp. Olive oil
Pinch of salt
Pinch of black pepper
Parsley, as much as desired
Enough flour to flour veal
Enough vegetable oil to fry veal

Place the vegetable oil in a frying pan and heat until it starts to bubble. In the meantime, flour the veal slices and place in hot oil. Fry on each side until golden brown. Take out of oil and set aside. Get rid of the vegetable oil from the pan but do not clean the pan. Place the olive oil and the butter in the pan. Cook until the butter has melted. Add the mushrooms. Cook on medium heat until the mushrooms are soft and golden brown. Add the salt, pepper, parsley and shrimps. Cook on medium heat for 2 minutes. Add the broccoli and sun dried tomatoes. Cook on medium heat for 1 minute. Add ½ cup broth, cream and the veal. Cook on medium heat for 5 minutes. If sauce begins to dry add some more broth. Flour the butter and add to the sauce. Cook on medium heat until the sauce is creamy, not watery. Serves 4 people.

Veal Macrì
Vitello alla Macrì

16 veal scallopini
1 lb. can tomato, crushed
8 slices Prosciutto cut in half
16 slices fontina or mozzarella cheese
1 small onion, finely chopped
1 garlic clove, finely chopped
½ cup vegetable oil
1 oz. butter
1 c. vegetable or veal broth
1 Tbsp. parsley, finely chopped
1 Tbsp. basil, finely chopped
½ tsp. oregano
½ tsp. salt
2 Tbsp. grated parmigian cheese
Enough flour to flour veal

Heat oven to 300°. Place onion, garlic and oil in frying pan (must not have a plastic handle because it will go in the oven). Cook on low heat until the onion and garlic are golden brown. Flour veal, add to the pan, and fry on low heat for 1 minute on each side. Add crushed tomatoes and cook on medium heat for 5 minutes. Add broth, butter, and seasonings; cook for 2 more minutes. Place prosciutto and the fontina on each slice of veal. Add parmigian cheese and some parsley for decoration. Remove from heat and place pan in oven until cheese is melted. Serves 4 people.

Veal Sorrento
Scaloppe Sorrentino

12 veal scallopini
1 large eggplant
1 lb. mozzarella, sliced
2 eggs
A pinch of salt
A pinch of black pepper
Enough flour to flour veal and eggplant
Enough vegetable oil to fry veal and eggplant
Parsley, finely chopped, enough for decoration
4 Tbsp. grated cheese
Marinara Sauce (see recipe)

Make marinara sauce (recipe in pasta section). Set aside. Heat oven to 350°. Place the vegetable oil in a frying pan and heat until it starts to bubble. In the meantime, flour the veal slices and place in hot oil. Fry on each side until golden brown. Peel and slice the eggplant into 8 (¼ inch) thick slices. Flour the eggplant. Set aside. Beat eggs and add salt and pepper. Pass the eggplant slices through the egg and place in the hot oil. Fry on each side until golden brown. Take out of oil, place on paper towel to drain out the excess oil and to cool off completely. Set aside. Place the veal into the marinara sauce and cook on medium heat for 1 minute. Take veal out of sauce. Cover the bottom of an oven proof dish with some marinara sauce. Place four slices of the eggplant (keeping the slices detached) on the sauce. Place three slices of veal on each eggplant slice and some more marinara sauce. Place the other four eggplant slices on top the veal. Cover the eggplant slices with marinara sauce. Place in oven for 2 minutes. Place mozzarella over eggplant slices. Sprinkle 1 tablespoon of grated cheese on each eggplant. Sprinkle some parsley over the cheese. Place back in oven until the mozzarella has melted and turned golden brown. Serves 4 people.

Veal Chop Cutlet
Cotoletta di Nodino

4 veal chops
6 large eggs
A pinch of salt
A pinch of black pepper
1 tsp. Parsley, finely chopped
½ tsp. oregano
1 tsp. basil, finely chopped
bread, enough to flour veal chops
Vegetable oil, enough to fry veal chops
1 lemon, cut into wedges

Bang veal chops (with the meat tenderizer) to flatten the meat. Beat eggs. Add salt, pepper, parsley, oregano and basil. Place veal chops in the flour and flour on both sides. Pass the veal chops through the eggs and then through the breadcrumbs. When well coated with breadcrumbs set aside. Heat oil until bubbles start to form around the edges. Place the veal chops in the frying pan. Fry on medium heat until golden brown. Turn and fry until golden brown. Take out and place on paper towel to drain excess oil. Serve with lemon wedges. Serves 4 people.

Veal Chops with Cherry Peppers
Nodino All'Agro

4 veal chops
8 jarred cherry peppers, cut into fourths
1 c. olive oil
A pinch of salt
A pinch of black pepper
1 garlic clove, finely chopped
1 small onion, finely chopped
1 c. veal broth
1 oz. butter
Enough flour to flour the veal chops

Place the veal chops on a platter, sprinkle the salt and pepper on both sides of the veal chops. Place the olive oil in a frying pan and heat until it starts to bubble. Flour the veal chops. Add to the frying pan; fry to your liking and golden brown on both sides. Add the cherry peppers, garlic and onion. Cook on medium heat until the onion becomes golden brown. Add the broth. Flour the butter and place in the broth. Cook on medium heat until the sauce has become creamy, not watery. Serves 4 people.

Veal Steak
Bistecca di Vitello

4 veal steaks
2 medium potatoes, boiled and cut very thin
1 c. roasted sweet peppers, sliced
1 c. vegetable oil
2 garlic cloves, finely chopped
1 small onion, finely chopped
1 tsp. rosemary
½ tsp. salt
A pinch of black pepper
1 tsp. oregano
1 tsp. parsley, finely chopped
1 tsp. basil, finely chopped

Place all ingredients in a container large enough to hold the four steaks. Place the steaks in the container. Let marinate for at least 30 minutes. Heat a frying pan for 2 minutes on low heat. Place the veal steaks in frying pan. Cook on medium heat until golden brown. Turnover. Cook on medium heat until the steak is cooked to your liking. Place on serving dishes. Pour the remaining oil over the steaks. Serves 4 people.

Veal and Peppers
Spezzatino di Vitello

2 lbs. veal stew
2 carrots, thinly chopped
2 celery stalks, thinly chopped
1 garlic clove, finely chopped
1 red sweet pepper
1 green sweet pepper
2 tsp. salt
2 pinches of black pepper
4 bay leaves
2 lb. can crushed tomato
½ c. olive oil
½ c. white wine
1 c. vegetable oil
¼ c. to ½ c. beef broth

Slice peppers to 1 inch wide pieces. Set aside. Place the vegetable oil in a frying pan and heat until it starts to bubble. Place the sweet peppers into the frying pan. Add ¼ teaspoon salt and a pinch of black pepper. Stir fry peppers on high heat for 5 minutes or until the peppers are soft and golden brown. When cooked drain peppers in a colander and set aside. Place the olive oil in a frying pan and heat until it starts to bubble. Add ¼ teaspoon salt, the carrots, celery and veal. Stir fry on medium heat until the veal starts turning golden brown. Add the white wine. Cook on medium heat until the veal is golden brown. Add the tomato, bay leaves, the rest of the salt and a pinch of black pepper. Cook on medium heat until the veal is cooked. If it becomes dry, add some more broth. Take out and throw away the bay leaves. Add the sweet peppers and mix well with the veal. Cook on medium heat for about 2 more minutes. Serves 4 people.

Veal Roast
Arrosto di Vitello

2 lb. veal roast
8 celery stalks, chopped
8 carrots, chopped
1 large onion, chopped
½ tsp. salt
A pinch of black pepper
4 sticks fresh rosemary or 1 Tbsp. crushed rosemary
2 to 3 cups veal broth
½ c. white wine
1 oz. butter
¼ c. vegetable oil

Heat oven to 350°. Sprinkle roast with salt and pepper. Place vegetable oil in frying pan. Heat oil until bubbles begin to form. Place roast, carrots, celery and onion in frying pan. Fry the meat on all sides until golden brown. Place the veal in an oven proof pan and pour the vegetable oil and vegetables over the top. Add the white wine and 2 cups of broth. Cover with aluminum foil and place in oven. Cook about 1 hour or until the veal is cooked. Adding more broth if needed.

Take out all of the vegetables and place in a blender or food processor. Process completely. Place the broth into a small pan. Add the processed vegetables to the broth in the small pan. Flour the butter and place in the sauce. Cook on medium heat until the sauce is creamy.

Cut the veal; place in four serving dishes and pour the sauce over the top. Serves 4 people.

Pork Dishes
Secondi di Maiale

Pork Chops with Tomatoes and Mozzarella Braciole con Pomadori e Mozzarella

4 large pork chops
4 small fresh tomatoes, cut to ½ inch pieces
8 slices of mozzarella
Enough flour to flour the pork chops
1 tsp. salt
A pinch of black pepper
½ tsp. Oregano
½ tsp. basil, finely chopped
½ tsp. parsley, finely chopped
1 small onion, finely chopped
2 garlic cloves, finely chopped
1 c. vegetable oil

Heat oven to 350°. Heat the vegetable oil until bubbles begin to form. Flour the pork chops and fry in hot oil on first side until golden brown. Turnover. Add the salt, pepper, onion, garlic, oregano, basil and parsley. Cook for 1 minute. Add the fresh tomatoes. Cook on medium heat for 5 minutes. Take pork chops out. Set aside. Pour the sauce into and oven proof dish. Place the pork chops over the sauce. Place the mozzarella over the pork chops. Place in oven until the mozzarella is melted. Serves 4 people.

Roast Pork with Milk
Arrosto di Maiale al latte

3 ½ lb. Roast Pork
herbs for roast, to your liking
Enough flour to flour the roast
1 c. vegetable oil
4 carrots, cut into ½ inch thick pieces
2 celery stalk, cut into ½ inch thick pieces
1 small onion, finely chopped
1 garlic clove, finely chopped
¼ tsp. salt
a pinch of black pepper
1 oz. Butter
1 c. broth
2 c. milk

Heat oven to 450°. Place roast on a serving platter and sprinkle the roast with herbs on all sides of the roast. Heat the vegetable oil in a frying pan until bubbles begin to form. Place the roast in the oil and fry on all sides until golden brown. Take the roast out of the frying pan. Place the roast in an oven proof pan. Do not get rid of the oil. Place the carrots, celery, garlic, onion, salt and black pepper in the oil used for the roast. Stir fry on medium heat for 5 minutes. Pour vegetables over roast. Place in oven and cook for ½ hour. Place a spear in the roast; if only clear juice comes out it is cooked, if not leave longer. Take vegetables out of pan, place in a blender and blend. Boil the milk and set aside. Place the blended vegetables in a medium sized pan. Flour the butter and add to the vegetables. Add the broth and milk to the vegetables. Cook on medium heat until sauce is creamy not watery. Slice the roast to ¾ inch thick slices and place in the sauce and cook on medium heat for 1to 2 minutes or just pour the sauce over the roast slices. Serves 4 people.

Pork Chops with Apples
Braciole alle Mele

4 large pork chops
½ tsp. rosemary, finely chopped
½ tsp. sage, finely chopped
½ tsp. basil, finely chopped
½ tsp. parsley, finely chopped
¼ tsp. salt
A pinch of black pepper
Any other herb that you like
1 c. vegetable oil
2 medium apples, peeled and thinly sliced
Enough flour to flour pork chops

Mix all the herbs together. Set aside. Place oil in a large frying pan, heat until bubbles begin to form. Flour the pork chops and place in the hot oil. Add half the herbs. Fry on medium heat until golden brown on first side. Turn the pork chops over. Add the apples and the rest of the herbs. Cook on medium heat until the pork chops are cooked. When cooked place the pork chops on serving dishes. Set aside. Cook the apples on medium heat for 1 more minute. Spoon the apples over the pork chops. Serves 4 people.

Chicken Dishes
Secondi di Pollo

Chicken Primavera
Pollo Primavera

4 large pieces of chicken breasts
4 to 6 beaten eggs
1 lb. breadcrumbs
2 bunches of arucola
20 cherry tomatoes, cut into fourths
8 Tbsp. olive oil
½ tsp. Salt
Juice of one lemon
1 Tbsp. basil, finely chopped
Enough flour to flour chicken breasts
Enough vegetable oil to fry chicken breasts

Wash, chop and dry arucola well. Place the arucola, cherry tomatoes, olive oil, salt, lemon juice and basil in a large dish. Mix well and set aside. Flatten the chicken, with a meat tenderizer, to ¼ inch thick pieces. Flour the chicken. Pass through the eggs and then place through the breadcrumbs. Do this process two times, so that you have about a ¾ inch thick chicken cutlet.

Place the vegetable oil in a frying pan and heat until it starts to bubble. Fry the chicken cutlets on both sides until golden brown. Place cutlets on paper towels to drain excess oil. Place in serving dishes and top with the arucola and cherry tomatoes mixture. Serves 4 people.

Pasquale Macrì

Chicken with Scallions
Pollo con Cipollotti

8 thin slices of chicken breast
4 scallions, chopped to 1 inch pieces
Juice of 1 large lemon
¼ tsp. salt
A pinch of black pepper
½ to 1 c. chicken broth
1 oz. butter
4 Tbsp. Olive oil
Enough vegetable oil to fry chicken
Enough flour to flour chicken

Heat vegetable oil in a large frying pan, until oil begins to bubble. Flour chicken and place in the hot oil. Fry on both sides until golden brown. Take chicken out of pan, throw out the vegetable oil but do not clean frying pan. Place olive oil in the frying pan. Add the scallions, salt and pepper. Cook on medium heat until the scallions are soft. Add the chicken and lemon juice. Cook on medium heat for 1 minute. Add ½ cup broth. Cook on medium heat for 5 minutes. Add more broth if sauce begins to dry. Flour the butter and add to the chicken. Cook on medium heat until the sauce is creamy, not watery. Serves 4 people.

Chicken Marsala
Pollo al Marsala

8 pieces of thin chicken breasts
1 c. mushrooms, sliced
½ c. of Marsala wine
1 oz. butter
1 Tbsp. olive oil
¼ tsp. salt
A pinch of black pepper
½ c. to 1 c. beef broth
1 oz. butter
Enough flour to flour chicken
Vegetable oil to fry chicken

Place the vegetable oil in a frying pan and heat until it starts to bubble. In the meantime flour the chicken breasts and place in hot oil. Fry on each side until golden brown. Take chicken out of pan and set aside. Place the olive oil, salt, pepper and mushrooms in the pan. Cook on medium heat until the mushrooms are soft and golden brown. Add the chicken back to the pan. Add the Marsala wine and cook on medium heat for 1 minute. Add ½ cup broth and cook on medium heat for 5 minutes. If sauce begins to dry add the rest of the broth. Flour the butter and add to the sauce. Cook on medium heat until the sauce is creamy, not watery. Serves 4 people.

Pasquale Macrì

Chicken Pasquale
Pollo alla Pasquale

8 thin chicken breasts
1 c. roasted peppers, sliced
1 c. mushrooms, sliced
1 c. canned artichokes
¼ tsp. salt
A pinch of black pepper
1 garlic clove, finely chopped
1 tsp. parsley, finely chopped
2 Tbsp. olive oil
½ c. to 1 c. beef broth
1 oz. butter
Enough flour to flour chicken
Enough vegetable oil to fry chicken

Place the vegetable oil in a frying pan and heat until it starts to bubble. In the meantime flour the chicken breasts and place in hot oil. Fry on each side until golden brown. Take out of oil and set aside. Get rid of the vegetable oil from the pan but do not clean the pan. Place the olive oil, garlic, salt, pepper, and parsley in the pan. Cook on medium heat for 1 minute. Add the mushrooms and artichokes. Cook on medium heat until the mushrooms are soft and golden brown. Add the roasted peppers and cook on medium heat for 1 minute. Add ½ cup broth and the chicken. Cook on medium heat for 5 minutes. If sauce begins to dry add the rest of the broth.

Flour the butter and add to the sauce. Cook on medium heat until the sauce is creamy, not watery. Serves 4 people.

Chicken Macrì
Pollo Macrì

8 thin pieces of chicken breasts
1 c. sun dried tomatoes
½ c. sherry wine
1 small onion, finely chopped
Pinch of salt
Pinch of black pepper
Pinch of oregano
1 tsp. parsley, finely chopped
1 c. broth
1 oz. butter
Enough flour to flour chicken
Enough vegetable oil to fry chicken

Place the vegetable oil in a frying pan and heat until it starts to bubble. In the meantime, flour the chicken and place in hot oil. Fry on each side until golden brown. Take out of oil and set aside. Place the onion in the pan. Cook on medium heat until the onion is golden brown. Take onion out of oil and set aside. Get rid of the vegetable oil from the pan but do not clean the pan.

Place the chicken and all the ingredients into the pan, except for the butter. Cook on medium heat for 5 minutes. Flour the butter and add to the pan. Cook on medium heat until the sauce is creamy, not watery. Serves 4 people.

Pasquale Macrì

The Chef's Chicken
Pollo dello Chef

8 thin slices of chicken breast
1 c. mushrooms, sliced
2 Tbsp. olive oil
8 oz. heavy cream
8 Tbsp. parmigian cheese
1 c. broth
1 oz. butter
A pinch of salt
A pinch of black pepper
Enough vegetable oil to fry chicken
Enough flour to flour chicken

Heat the vegetable oil in a large frying pan, until the oil begins to bubble. Flour the chicken and add to the hot oil. Fry on both sides until golden brown. Take the chicken out. Throw out the oil but do not clean the frying pan. Add the olive oil to the pan. Add the mushrooms, salt and pepper. Cook on medium heat until the mushrooms are soft. Add the broth and cook on medium heat for 5 minutes. Add the parmigian cheese. Cook on medium heat for 1 minute. Add the heavy cream and cook on medium heat for 3 minutes. Flour the butter and add to the sauce. Cook on medium heat for 2 more minutes or until the sauce is creamy. Serves 4 people.

Chicken and Potatoes
Pollo con Patate

8 thin pieces of chicken breasts
4 medium fresh tomatoes, chopped
2 large potatoes, thinly sliced
1 red sweet pepper, thinly sliced
1 small onion, thinly sliced
½ tsp. salt
A pinch of black pepper
1 tsp. oregano
4 Tbsp. olive oil
Enough vegetable oil to fry chicken
Enough flour to flour chicken

Heat vegetable oil in large frying pan until oil begins to bubble. Flour chicken and place in hot oil. Fry on each side until golden brown. Take chicken out of pan. Throw out the vegetable oil but do not clean the frying pan. Place the olive oil in the frying pan. Add the potatoes, red peppers, onion, black pepper and oregano. Cook on medium heat for about 5 minutes or until the potatoes become soft. Add the salt, tomatoes and chicken to the pan. Cook on medium heat for 5 more minutes or until the tomatoes become a light sauce. Serves 4 people.

Turkey Dishes
Secondi di Tacchino

Turkey in a Butter and Sage Sauce
Tacchino con Burro e Salvia

8 thin slices turkey breasts
4 oz. Butter
8 fresh sage leaves
½ tsp. Salt
Pinch of black pepper
Enough flour to flour the turkey
Enough vegetable oil to fry the turkey

Place the vegetable oil in a frying pan and heat until it starts to bubble. In the meantime flour the turkey breasts and place in hot oil. Fry on each side until golden brown. Take out of oil and set aside. Get rid of the vegetable oil from the pan but do not clean the pan. Place the butter in the pan and let it melt. Add the sage, salt, pepper and turkey. Cook on low heat for about 5 minutes.

Place the turkey into serving dishes. Pour the butter and sage sauce over the turkey. Serves 4 people.

Turkey with Almonds and Walnuts
Tacchino Mandorle e Noci

8 thin slices of turkey breast
1 c. almonds, thinly chopped
1 c. walnuts, thinly chopped
Salt
Pinch of black pepper
Enough flour to flour turkey breasts
8 to 10 oz. butter

Mix the almonds and walnuts in a deep dish. Sprinkle the salt and pepper over the turkey breasts. Pass the turkey breasts through the almond and walnut mixture. Pat well so that the almond and walnut mixture sticks to the turkey. Melt the butter in a large non-stick frying pan. Flour the turkey breasts and place in the frying pan. Add any remaining almond and walnut mixture. Cook on medium heat until golden brown on both sides of the turkey breasts, approximately 3 minutes on each side. Place on serving dishes and drizzle over the remaining butter, almonds and walnuts. Serves 4 people.

Pasquale Macrì

Rolled Turkey
Involtini di Tacchino

8 thin slices of turkey breasts
8 slices of pastrami or prosciutto
8 slices of fontina or mozzarella cheese
8 sage leaves
2 tsp. parsley, finely chopped
salt
Pinch of black pepper
4 tsp. grated cheese
Enough flour to flour turkey breasts
Enough vegetable oil to fry turkey breasts
2 oz. butter
½ c. beer
½ to 1 c. broth
Potato Puree

Place the turkey breasts on a flat surface. Place a slice of pastrami, a slice of cheese, 1 sage leaf, ¼ tsp. parsley, and ½ tsp. grated cheese in each slice of turkey. Roll inwards and close with a string. Place the vegetable oil in a frying pan and heat until it starts to bubble. In the meantime flour the rolled turkey and place in hot oil. Fry on each side until golden brown. Take out of oil and set aside. Get rid of the vegetable oil from the pan but do not clean the pan. Place the 1 ounce butter, the rolled turkey, a pinch of salt and a pinch of black pepper in the pan. Cook on low heat until the butter is melted. Add the beer. Cook on medium heat until beer has evaporated. Add ½ cup broth and cook on medium heat for 5 minutes. If sauce begins to dry add the rest of the broth. Flour the remaining butter and add to the sauce. Cook on medium heat until the sauce is creamy, not watery. Place in serving dishes and serve with your favorite potato puree and a sage leaf for decoration. Serves 4 people.

Seafood Dishes
Secondi di Pesce

Mixed Seafood Grilled
Misto Griglia

8 cleaned squid
2 swordfish steaks, cut in half
2 salmon steaks, cut in half
2 doz. Large shrimp
1 lb. monkfish
1 doz. Scallops
Any other fish that you like
Salt
Black pepper
1 oz. vegetable oil
2 oz. olive oil
Parsley, finely chopped
Grilled vegetables (Antipasti)
2 lemons cut into wedges

Heat flat grill or a barbecue for half an hour before placing the fish on it. Place all of the fish on a large platter; sprinkle the fish with a pinch of salt and a pinch of black pepper. Drizzle the vegetable oil over the top. Place on hot grill. Cook about 3 minutes on each side. Or until cooked depending on how hot the grill is. Place in serving dishes, place grilled vegetables around the fish. Add a bit of salt to each dish. Drizzle some olive oil over the fish. Decorate with parsley. Serve with lemon wedges. Serves 4 people.

Sea Bass Baked in Salt
Branzino al Sale

4 ½ lb. sea bass or sea bream
2 to 4 lbs. Coarse Salt (enough to cover fish)
2 oz olive oil
Parsley for decoration
2 Lemons cut into wedges

Clean out the sea bass or have it done at the fish market, but leave the sea bass whole and with skin intact. Heat oven to 350°. Place the sea bass in a deep oven pan. Cover with salt. Cover with aluminum foil. Place in oven and bake for 30 minutes (if the sea bass is larger let it cook longer). Take off aluminum foil and bake for 5 more minutes. Take off the salt and discard.

Place the sea bass in serving dishes as is or make into filets. Drizzle with the olive oil and parsley. Serve with lemon wedges. Serves 4 people.

Grilled Seafood Primavera
Pesce Primavera

4 swordfish filets or other fish filets
A pinch of salt
Pinch black pepper
¼ c. vegetable oil
30 to 40 cherry tomatoes
4 bunches arucola
¼ c. olive oil
1 tsp. salt
Pinch of black pepper
1 tsp. basil, finely chopped
¼ tsp. oregano
Juice of ½ a lemon

Heat flat grill or barbecue on high heat for 10 minutes; if barbecue grill keep flame on medium.

Place filets on dish and drizzle with oil and add salt and pepper. Set aside. Wash and cut tomatoes into fourths. Wash and chop the arucola. Set aside to dry well. Mix together tomatoes, arucola, and all other ingredients. Set aside. Grill filets 3 to 5 minutes or until light brown on each side. Place filets on serving dishes and spoon sauce on the filets and serve. Serves 4 people.

Sole Fish in a Lemon and Wine Sauce
Sogliola alla Mugnaia

8 filets of sole fish or monkfish
2 oz. butter
½ c. white wine
Juice of 2 lemons
¼ tsp. salt
A pinch of black pepper
1 c. fish broth
Enough flour to flour the filets
Enough vegetable oil to fry filets
Parsley, finely chopped

Place the vegetable oil in a frying pan and heat until it starts to bubble. In the meantime, flour the sole fish and place in hot oil. Fry on each side until golden brown. Take out of oil and set aside. Get rid of the vegetable oil from the pan but do not clean the pan. Place 1 ounce butter, salt, pepper, lemon juice and white wine in the pan. Cook on medium heat for 2 minutes.

Add the broth and the sole fish. Flour the remaining butter and add to the sauce. Cook on medium heat until the sauce is creamy, not watery. Place the sole fish in serving dishes. Pour the sauce over and decorate with the parsley. Serves 4 people.

Baked Swordfish with Arucola
Tagliata di Spada con Rucola

1 lb. swordfish chunk (or 1 lb. salmon)
½ c. olive oil
A pinch of salt
A pinch of black pepper
1 tsp. parsley, finely chopped
Lemon wedges

Heat oven to 350°. Wash, cut and drain arucola. Set aside. Oil the bottom of an oven proof dish with the ½ cup olive oil. Set aside. Slice the swordfish or salmon to ½ inch slices and place over the olive oil in the pan. Add the salt, pepper and parsley. Place in the oven and bake for 10 to 15 minutes. Place in serving dishes and place the arucola over the top. Serve with lemon wedges. Serves 4 people.

Swordfish with Porcini Mushrooms
Tagliata di Spada ai Porcini

1 lb. swordfish chunk
½ c. olive oil
2 c. porcini mushrooms – sliced
1 garlic clove – finely chopped
2 Tbsp. olive oil
A pinch of salt
A pinch of black pepper
1 tsp. parsley
1 shot of white wine

Heat oven to 350°. Oil the bottom of an oven proof dish with the ½ cup olive oil. Set aside.

Slice the swordfish to ½ inch slices and place over the olive oil in the pan. Set aside. Place the 2 tablespoons olive oil, garlic and mushrooms in a frying pan. Cook on medium heat for 1 minute.

Add the salt, pepper and white wine. Cook on medium heat until the mushrooms are golden brown. Spoon the mushrooms over the swordfish and add the parsley. Place in the oven and bake for 10 to 15 minutes. Serves 4 people.

White Sicilian Swordfish
Spada Siciliana-In Bianco

4 swordfish steaks
2 doz. Medium sized shrimp
1 garlic clove, finely chopped
1 small onion, finely chopped
½ oz. butter
1 c. black olives, sliced
2 Tbsp. capers
4 anchovies
½ tsp. parsley, finely chopped
¼ tsp oregano
A pinch of salt
A pinch of black pepper
1 c. olive oil
½ c. white wine
½ c. to 1 c. vegetable or fish broth
Enough flour to flour swordfish

Place the olive oil in a frying pan and heat until it starts to bubble. Lightly flour swordfish. Place the swordfish into the hot oil and fry on each side until golden brown. Take out and set aside. Add the onion and garlic to the olive oil. Stir fry until golden brown. Add the olives, capers and anchovies. Cook on medium heat for 1 minute. Add the shrimp and white wine. Cook on medium heat for 1 minute. Add the salt, pepper, parsley and oregano. Cook on medium heat for 1 more minute. Add the swordfish and ½ cup broth. Flour the butter and add to the sauce. Cook on medium until the sauce becomes creamy, not watery. If sauce starts to dry add more broth. Serves 4 people.

Swordfish in a Red Sauce
Spada Siciliana

4 swordfish steaks
2 doz. Medium shrimps
1 garlic clove, finely chopped
1 small onion, finely chopped
½ oz. butter
4 fresh tomatoes, finely chopped
1 c. black olives, sliced
2 Tbsp. Capers
4 to 8 anchovies
A pinch of salt
A pinch of black pepper
¼ c. olive oil
A shot of white wine
¼ c. vegetable or fish broth
½ c. vegetable oil
Enough flour to flour seafood

Place the vegetable oil in a frying pan and heat until it starts to bubble. Lightly flour the swordfish and shrimps. Place the swordfish and shrimps into the hot oil and fry on each side until golden brown. Take out and set aside. Get rid of oil but do not clean pan. Place the butter, olive oil, onion, and garlic in the pan. Stir fry until golden brown. Add the fresh tomatoes and the white wine. Cook on medium heat for 1 minute. Add the olives, capers, anchovies, salt and black pepper. Cook on medium heat for 1 minute. Add the swordfish and shrimps. Cook on medium heat for 5 minutes or until the swordfish is cooked. If the sauce becomes dry add some broth. Serves 4 people.

Pasquale Macrì

Filled Squid
Calamari Ripiene

10 oz. breadcrumbs
½ tsp. parsley, finely chopped
½ tsp. basil, finely chopped
1 garlic clove, finely chopped
¼ tsp. salt
¼ tsp. black pepper
2 to 4 oz. white wine
2 to 4 oz. olive oil
40 medium (30-40 size) squid

Heat oven to 500°. Boil calamari in unsalted water for 5 minutes, then drain. Set aside to cool off. Mix all filling ingredients; must be wet but still crumbly. Fill calamari. Oil oven pan.

Bake for 15 minutes or until golden brown. Serves 4 people.

Shrimp Macrì
Gamberoni alla Macrì

2 doz. Large shrimps
1 c. roasted peppers, sliced
1 c. mushrooms sliced
4 to 8 slices anchovies, chopped
Enough flour to flour shrimps
Enough vegetable oil to fry shrimps
1 garlic clove, finely chopped
1 small onion, finely chopped
1 Tbsp. olive oil
½ c. white wine
½ c. to 1 c. fish broth
1 oz. butter

Place the vegetable oil in a frying pan and heat until it starts to bubble. In the meantime, flour the shrimps and place in hot oil. Fry on each side until golden brown. Take out of oil and set aside. Get rid of the vegetable oil from the pan but do not clean the pan. Place the olive oil, garlic, onion and mushrooms in the pan. Cook on medium heat until the mushrooms are soft and golden brown. Add the roasted peppers and cook on medium heat for 1 minute. Add the anchovies and cook on medium heat for 30 seconds. Add the shrimp and white wine. Cook on medium heat until white wine has evaporated. Add ½ cup broth and cook on medium heat for 5 minutes. If sauce begins to dry add the rest of the broth. Flour the butter and add to the sauce. Cook on medium heat until the sauce is creamy, not watery. Serves 4 people.

Pasquale Macrì

Shrimp Pasquale
Gamberoni alla Pasquale

2 doz. Large shrimps
4 large tomatoes, chopped
1 small onion, finely chopped
½ garlic clove, finely chopped
1 Tbsp. olive oil
¼ tsp. parsley, finely chopped
½ tsp. basil, finely chopped
Pinch of salt
¼ c. white wine
Juice of 1 lemon
1 oz. butter
Enough flour to flour shrimps
Enough vegetable oil to fry shrimps

Place the vegetable oil in a frying pan and heat until it starts to bubble. In the meantime, flour the shrimps and place in hot oil. Fry on each side until golden brown. Take out of oil and set aside. Get rid of the vegetable oil from the pan but do not clean the pan. Place the olive oil, garlic, onion, salt, black pepper, parsley, basil and fresh tomatoes in the pan. Cook on medium heat for 5 minutes. Add the white wine and the lemon juice. Cook on medium heat for 5 more minutes. Add the shrimp and if dry add some water. Cook for 2 minutes. Flour the butter and add to the sauce. Cook on medium heat for 2 minutes after that the butter has melted. Serves 4.

Monkfish in a Red Sauce
Pescatrice Rossa

4 large filets of sole fish or monkfish
16 large scallops
16 large shrimps
Marinara sauce (recipe in the pasta section)
Enough olive oil to lightly oil 2 inch deep pan

Make marinara sauce and set aside. Heat oven to 350°. Oil just the bottom of the pan. Place a little of the sauce over the oil. Place the filets in the pan about 4 inches apart. Place the scallops and shrimp over the filets. Cover the fish with the marinara sauce and place in the oven. Bake 15 to 20 minutes. Serves 4 people.

Monkfish with Saffron
Pescatrice allo Zafferano

2 lbs. monkfish
Juice of 1 large lemon
½ c. white wine
2 oz. butter
¼ tsp. saffron
1 c. fish broth
Enough vegetable oil to fry monkfish
Enough flour to flour monkfish

Place the vegetable oil in a frying pan and heat until it starts to bubble. In the meantime, flour the monkfish and place in hot oil. Fry on each side until golden brown. Take out of oil and set aside. Do not clean the pan. Place 1 ounce butter, white wine, lemon juice, broth and saffron in the pan. Cook on medium heat for 3 minutes. Add the monkfish to the sauce. Flour the remaining butter and add to the sauce. Cook until creamy, not watery. Serves 4 people.

Salmon with Butter and Sage
Salmone Burro e Salvia

4 salmon steaks
4 oz. Butter
8 fresh stems sage
Pinch of salt
Pinch of black pepper
Enough flour to flour the salmon
Enough vegetable oil to fry salmon

Place the vegetable oil in a frying pan and heat until it starts to bubble. In the meantime, flour the salmon steaks and place in hot oil. Fry on each side until golden brown. Take out of oil and set aside. Get rid of the vegetable oil from the pan but do not clean the pan. Place the butter in the pan and let it melt. Add the sage, salt, pepper and salmon. Cook on medium heat for about 5 minutes or until the salmon is cooked. Put the salmon in serving dishes. Pour the butter and sage over the salmon. Serves 4 people.

Salmon in an Amaretto Sauce
Salmone All'Amaretto

4 salmon steaks
¼ c. amaretto
10 oz. heavy cream
¼ c to ½ c. fish broth
2 oz. Butter
¼ c. Sliced almonds
Pinch of salt
Pinch of black pepper
Enough flour to flour the salmon
Enough vegetable oil to fry salmon
1 orange, cut into ¼ inch slices leaving the peel on (for decoration)
Just the peel of an eggplant, julienne (for decoration)

Place the vegetable oil in a frying pan and heat until it starts to bubble. In the meantime, flour the salmon steaks and place in hot oil. Fry on each side until golden brown. Take out of oil and set aside. Place the vegetable oil in a small frying pan. Do not clean the pan that the salmon was fried in. Place the butter and almonds in the pan that was used to fry the salmon. Cook until the almonds are golden brown. Add the salt, pepper, amaretto and salmon. Cook on medium heat for 3 minutes or until the amaretto has evaporated. Add the cream and ¼ cup broth. Cook on low heat until creamy. In the meantime, place the orange slices and eggplant julienne in the left over vegetable oil. Stir fry until golden brown. Take out of oil and drain on a paper towel. Put the salmon in serving dishes. Pour the sauce over the salmon steaks. Decorate with the orange and eggplant slices. Serves 4 people.

Vegetable Dishes
Secondi di Verdura

Asparagus Parmigian
Asparagi alla Parmigiana

40 spears of asparagus (if fresh cut off ends of spears if too thick)
12 slices mozzarella
Tomato Sauce (recipe in pasta section)
8 Tbsp. grated parmigian cheese
2 Tbsp salt.
Parsley, finely chopped

Heat oven to 400°. Tie the asparagus into batches (10 per batch). Place asparagus in a large pan and cover with water. Add salt. Bring to a boil and cook for 10 to 15 minutes or until the asparagus are cooked. In two baking pans put enough tomato sauce to cover bottom, then make 4 parms by placing 10 spears next to each other in the pan. Put tomato sauce over the top. Place the mozzarella slices over the spears, covering them completely. Top each with 2 tablespoons of cheese and parsley. Place in oven until mozzarella is melted and lightly browned. Serves 4 people.

Asparagus with Eggs
Asparagi alla Bismarc

20 asparagus spears
8 eggs
1 Tbsp. salt
4 to 8 Tbsp. grated cheese
3 oz. Butter

Tie the asparagus into batches (5 per batch). Place asparagus in a large pan and cover with water. Add salt. Bring to a boil and cook for 10 to 15 minutes or until the asparagus are cooked. Do not over cook. Place butter in a non stick frying pan. Cook the eggs on low heat, sunny side up. Place the asparagus on a serving platter; place the eggs on top. Pour the butter over the eggs and sprinkle with the grated cheese. Serves 4 people.

Pasquale Macrì

Eggplant Parmigian
Melanzana alla Parmigiana

Marinara Sauce (recipe in pasta section)
2 large eggplants
40 slices of mozzarella
4 eggs
A pinch of salt
A pinch of black pepper
8 tsp. grated cheese
Enough flour to flour eggplant slices
Enough vegetable oil to fry eggplant slices

Make marinara sauce. Set aside. Peel and slice eggplant into 20 (¼ inch thick) slices. Pass each slice of eggplant through the flour and set aside. Beat eggs and add salt and pepper. Put oil in frying pan; heat on high heat until oil starts to bubble. Lower the heat to medium. Pass the eggplant slices through the egg and place in the hot oil. Fry on each side until golden brown on each side. Take out of oil; place on paper towel to drain out the excess oil and to cool off completely. Heat oven to 350°. Cover bottom of an oven proof dish with the a thin layer of marinara sauce. Place eggplant slices two 9 X 13 X 2 inch pans in 4 separate pieces. Cover each eggplant slice with sauce, 1 teaspoon grated cheese and 1 slice of mozzarella; cover with another eggplant slice and continue the process until there are no more eggplant slices. Do not add the mozzarella on the top slice. Cover pans with aluminum foil and place in oven for 15 minutes. Take the cover off of the pans; cover each eggplant slice with mozzarella. Place in oven again for 5 minutes or until mozzarella is melted and golden brown. Serves 4 people.

Side Dishes
Contorni

Escarole and Beans
Scarola e Fagioli

- 4 c. escarole, boiled and salted
- 16. oz. Cannellini beans
- 2 Tbsp. Olive oil
- 1 oz. butter
- 2 to 4 garlic cloves, finely chopped
- 4 Tbsp. breadcrumbs
- 4 Tbsp. grated cheese
- 1 tsp. parsley, finely chopped
- 1 tsp. basil, finely chopped
- 1 tsp. oregano

Heat oven or broiler to 350°. Place the breadcrumbs, grated cheese, parsley, basil and oregano in a small bowl; mix well. Set aside. Place the butter, olive oil and garlic in a frying pan. Stir fry on low heat until garlic is golden brown. Add the escarole and cook on medium heat for 3 minutes. Add the cannellini beans and cook on medium heat for 1 minute. Place in an oven proof pan. Sprinkle the breadcrumbs mixture over the top. Place under the broiler or in the oven until golden brown. Serves 4 people.

Baked Broccoli
Broccoli Gratinati

- 4 c. broccoli, boiled and salted
- 4 Tbsp. olive oil
- 1 garlic clove, finely chopped
- ½ oz. butter
- ¼ tsp. crushed hot pepper (optional)
- 4 Tbsp. breadcrumbs
- 4 Tbsp. grated cheese
- 1 tsp. parsley, finely chopped
- 1 tsp. basil, finely chopped
- 1 tsp. oregano

Heat oven to 350°. Mix the breadcrumbs, cheese, parsley, basil and oregano in a small bowl. Set aside. Place the garlic, hot pepper, olive oil and butter in a frying pan until the butter has melted. Add the broccoli and cook on medium heat for 5 minutes, stirring occasionally. Place the broccoli in a oven proof pan. Place the breadcrumb mixture over the top. Place the broccoli in the oven and bake for about 10 minutes or until golden brown. Serves 4 people.

Breaded Fennel
Finocchi Gratinati

8 medium fennel
½ c. olive oil
1 garlic clove, finely chopped
A pinch of black pepper
2 c. milk
2 oz. Butter
1 oz. Flour
¼ tsp. Salt
A pinch of black pepper
A pinch of nut meg
4 Tbsp. grated cheese
4 Tbsp. breadcrumbs

Boil milk with ¼ teaspoon salt, a pinch black pepper and nut meg. Take off film that has formed on milk. In another small pan melt butter on low heat; don't burn. Constantly stirring sprinkle flour over butter. When creamy, not crumbly, add milk all at once. Continue stirring until it begins to thicken. Take off heat. Set aside to cool completely, stirring occasionally. Heat oven to 350°. Wash the fennels, cut off the stems and place in a pan and cover with water. Salt water to your liking. Cook fennels on high heat until you can pass a fork through them without any problems. Drain; let cool and slice to ½ inch slices and set aside. Place olive oil and garlic in a frying pan. When oil starts to bubble add the fennel. Add the black pepper and cook on medium heat until the fennel is golden brown. Place the fennel in an oven proof pan.

Pour the sauce over the fennel. Sprinkle the grated cheese over the sauce. Place in hot oven until golden brown. Serves 4 people.

Pasquale Macrì

Sautéed Spinach
Spinaci Saltati

4 c. spinach (or any green leaf vegetable), boiled and salted
4 Tbsp. olive oil
½ oz. butter
2 garlic cloves, finely chopped
1 Tbsp. grated cheese

Place the butter, olive oil and garlic in frying pan. Stir fry on low heat until garlic is golden brown. Add the spinach and cheese. Sauté on medium heat for 2 minutes. Serves 4 people.

Desserts
Dolce

Chocolate Salami
Salame di Cioccolata

6 oz. butter, softened
2 oz. bitter cocoa powder
8 oz. sugar
10 oz. biscuits
1 egg
1 shot of grappa (Italian distilled liquor)
1 oz. almonds
1 oz. hazelnuts

Crush cookies in a food processor until finely crushed. Take out of food processor and set aside.

Place butter, cocoa, sugar, egg and grappa in food processor. Process until well mixed. Add to the cookies. Set aside. Place the almonds and hazelnuts in the food processor and process until coarsely chopped. Add to the cookies and mix well with wooden spoon. Mix well. Place dough on plastic wrap. Work with hands until a 2 inch diameter and 15 inch long roll is formed. Tightly wrap in the plastic wrap. Place in refrigerator and leave overnight. When ready, slice into ½ inch thick slices. Serve with whipped cream or as is. Store in refrigerator in plastic wrap.

Cooked Cream Panna Cotta

7 oz. heavy cream
7 oz. milk
4 g. gelatin sheets
2 tsp. vanilla
2 oz. confectioner's sugar
1 c. cold water
1 Tbsp. rum
your favorite topping (strawberry, chocolate, caramel etc.)

Add the rum to the water. Place the gelatin sheet in the water and let sit for 10 minutes. Place the heavy cream, milk and vanilla in a small pan. Place on medium heat; bring to a boil. Add the confectioner's sugar and stirring constantly cook on medium heat for 1 more minute. Drain the gelatin sheets. Add the gelatin sheets to the cream mixture. Pour into 4 molds and let stand at room temperature for 1 hour. Place in refrigerator for at least 5 hours. Top with your favorite topping or with fresh fruit. Serve cold.

Caramelized Cream
Crème Caramel

2 c. milk
1 c. heavy cream
3 eggs
9 oz. sugar
¼ tsp. anisette
lemon zest of ½ a lemon
9 aluminum cupcake cups

Put 4 ounces of sugar in a small non stick pan and cook over medium heat until caramel is formed (watch closely so that it does not burn). Pour about 1 teaspoon of the hot caramel into the aluminum cups; turn the cup around until the bottom is covered with the caramel (be careful not to get burned because the cups are hot). Then set the cups aside. Heat oven to 350°. Put the milk, heavy cream, lemon zests and anisette in a small pan and cook on medium heat. Bring milk to a boil and stirring constantly boil for 1 minute. Remove from heat and add the remaining 5 ounces of sugar; stir until melted. Beat and add the eggs one at a time to the milk, stirring briskly with a whisk. Take out the lemon zests. Using a drainer, pour the mixture in the aluminum cups to ¾ full. Place a sheet of old newspaper on the bottom of a pan that is large enough to hold all the cups. The pan must also be as deep as the aluminum cups. Add about 1 cup of water over the newspaper. Place the aluminum cups in the pan and make sure that the water in the pan covers the bottom of the aluminum cups to about ½ way. Place in the oven and bake for 30 minutes or until set. Do not overcook. Take out of oven and let them cool off completely. Refrigerate for at least 3 hours before serving. To serve, turn upside down on a small dish. These can be kept in the refrigerator up to 5 days.

Pick Me Up
Tiramisù

1 lb. mascarpone cheese
48 savoiardi cookies (finger cookies)
2 Tbsp. heavy cream
2 Tbsp. cocoa powder
6 eggs
7 Tbsp. sugar
enough espresso coffee to dip cookies in
4 oz. unsweetened chocolate

Make espresso coffee and set aside to cool off. Place mascarpone, heavy cream and 1 tablespoon of cocoa powder in a large dish. Mix with a electric mixer until smooth, then set aside. Separate eggs. Place yolks and whites in two medium sized bowls. Wash and dry the mixer whisks very well. Add sugar to egg yolks and mix on maximum speed until lemon colored, fluffy and smooth. Then set aside. Wash and dry mixer whisks very well. Mix egg whites on high speed until stiff peaks are formed. Then set aside. Add yolk mixture to the mascarpone mixture and mix on maximum speed until well blended. Fold egg whites into the mixture very slowly with a wooden spoon until well blended. Then place cream in refrigerator. Dip cookies quickly in coffee. (Do not leave in the coffee). Place the cookies in the bottom of a glass pan or in individual fruit dishes. Pour the cream mixture over the cookies. Sprinkle the remaining cocoa powder over the cream. Shave the chocolate with a potato peeler and place chocolate shavings over the cream. Refrigerate for a maximum of 2 days. This dessert can be frozen. Take out 2 hours before serving.

Limoncello Cake
Torta al Limoncello

2 sponge cake discs
14 oz. mascarpone cheese
½ c. limoncello or your favorite liquor
7 oz. confectioner's sugar
2 Tbsp. flour
4 egg yolks
2 c. heavy cream
2 oz. confectioner's sugar
grated lemon zest
Your favorite fresh fruit

In a small bowl stir together the mascarpone and ¼ cup of limoncello. Set aside. In a large bowl mix together the yolks and the confectioner's sugar until yellow and well mixed. Add the lemon zest. Stir the mascarpone mixture into the egg mixture with a wooden spoon. Set aside. Mix together on maximum speed the heavy cream and sugar until whipped cream is formed. Place the whipped cream in a pastry bag. Place in refrigerator for 30 minutes. Brush the sponge cake with the remaining limoncello. Place ¾ of the mascarpone filling on the first sponge cake disc. Place the second disc on top of the filling. Then top with the remaining filling. Now pipe the whipped cream all around the cake. Decorate with fresh fruit to your liking.

Short Crust Pastry I
Pasta Frolla I

FOR A 9 INCH PIE
2 ½ c. flour
1 tsp. baking powder
4 oz. butter, cold, cut into small pieces
¾ c. sugar
1 egg
1 egg yolk
pinch of salt

Sift the flour. Add salt and baking powder; mix well. Set aside. Work the sugar and butter quickly with your hands until the mixture well blended. Incorporate the flour mixture. Add the egg and the egg yolk. Knead well with hands until a soft but not sticky dough is formed. Roll dough into a ball and place in the refrigerator for 30 minutes. Grease and flour the bottom of a 9 inch layer cake pan. Roll out, on a floured surface, 2/3 of the dough to a 13 inch round circle. Place on the bottom and 1 inch up the sides of the pan. You are now ready to fill with your favorite filling. Roll out remaining dough. Set aside.

Short Crust Pastry II
Pasta Frolla II

FOR A 9 INCH TART
1 ¼ c. flour
½ tsp. baking powder
3 ½ oz. oz. butter, cold, cut into small pieces
½ c. sugar
1 egg yolk
pinch of salt

Sift the flour. Add salt and baking powder; mix well. Set aside. Work the sugar and butter quickly with your hands until the mixture is well blended. Incorporate the flour mixture. Add the egg yolk. Knead well with hands until a soft but not sticky dough is formed. Roll dough into a ball and place in the refrigerator for 30 minutes. Grease and flour the bottom of a 9 inch pie pan. Roll out, on a floured surface to a 13 inch round circle. Place in the pie pan. You are now ready to fill with your favorite filling.

Pastry Cream
Crema Pasticcera

FOR A 9 INCH PIE
4 egg yolks
¾ c. milk
2 c. flour
6 oz. sugar
¼ tsp. vanilla
zest of ½ lemon
zest of 1/ orange

Place the flour in a medium sized bowl. Whisk enough milk into the flour so that it is smooth (approximately ¼ cup). Set aside. Beat the egg yolks. Whisk into the flour. Set aside. Place the remaining milk, sugar, vanilla and zests into a large pan. Stir until the sugar is melted. Place over medium heat and bring to a boil. Take off of heat and drain in to a large glass bowl. (This is done to eliminate the zests and any milk layers.) Wash the pan well. Sieve the flour mixture into the milk. Pour the mixture back into the large pan. Cook on medium heat, stirring constantly with the whisk until the cream is formed. (Being careful that it does not burn.) Take off of heat. Pour back into large glass bowl. Let the cream cool completely. Stirring occasionally, so that a film does not form. When completely cooled, cover with plastic wrap and refrigerate until needed.

Chocolate Cream

Follow recipe above. When completely cooled, add ¼ cup of cocoa powder and mix well.

Pine Nut and Cream Cake
Torta della Nonna

Crust (see short crust I recipe)
Pastry Cream (see recipe)
¼ c. pine nuts
3 Tbsp. milk
Confectioner's sugar for decoration

Make pastry cream according to recipe. Set aside. Heat the oven to 350°. Grease and flour a 9 inch layer cake pan. Place the dough into the pan. Fill the dough with the pastry cream. Place the remaining dough over the cream. Make sure that the pie is closed well or the cream will over flow. Brush the dough with the milk. Place the pine nuts on top of the dough. Place in the oven. Bake for 30 minutes or until golden brown. Cool on a cooling rack for 15 minutes. Take out of the pan. Cool off completely. Sprinkle with confectioner's sugar.

Fruit Tort
Crostata di Frutta

Tart Crust (see recipe)
Pastry cream (see recipe)
4 Tbsp. apricot jelly
Strawberries
Kiwis
Mandarins
Pineapples
Grapes

Make cream according to recipe. Set aside. Heat the oven to 350°. Grease and flour a 9 inch pie pan. Make crust according to recipe. Place the dough is in the pan. Using a fork, poke holes all over the dough, bottom and sides. Place in oven and bake for 20 to 30 minutes or until the crust is golden brown. Let the crust cool off on a cooling rack for 15 minutes. Take out of pan. Let the crust cool off completely before filling with cream. When the crust has cooled off, place the cream into the crust and refrigerate for 30 minutes before adding the fruit. In the meantime, wash and dry your favorite fruit. Slice the fruit into ½ inch thick pieces. Place the fruit over the cream alternating to make into a colorful pie. Heat the apricot jelly and sieve. With a pastry brush, brush the hot apricot jelly over the fruit. Refrigerate for 30 minutes before use.

Ricotta Pie
Crostata di Ricotta

Crust (see short crust recipe II)
1 lb. ricotta
1 ¼ c. confectioner's sugar
4 oz. candied fruit
pinch of cinnamon
4 egg yolks

Heat the oven to 350°. Grease and flour an 8 inch pie pan. Make crust according to recipe. Place the crust into the pan. Set aside. Place the ricotta in a large bowl. Mix the ricotta with a hand mixer on medium speed for about 1 minute or until the ricotta is smooth. Add the egg yolks, one at a time, mixing well after each yolk is added. Add all other ingredients. Mix well until smooth. Pour into pan. Cut off excess dough. Leaving about ¼ inch dough above the filling. Roll out the excess dough. Using a fluted wheel, cut the dough into ½ inch wide strips. Place over the filling. Brush the strips with milk. Bake for 30 minutes. Let the pie cool off on a cooling rack for 15 minutes. Take out of pan and let the pie cool off completely. Sprinkle with confectioner's sugar.

Chocolate and Pear Pie
Crostata di Pere e Cioccolata

Crust (see short crust recipe I)
Chocolate Pastry Cream (see recipe)
1 Large Pear, cut into ½ inch cubes

Heat oven to 350°. Grease and flour a 8 inch layer cake pan. Make cream according to recipe. Add the pears to the chocolate cream. Mix well. Set Aside. Make dough according to recipe. Place the bottom dough in the layer cake pan. Set aside. Pour the cream into the crust. Place the top dough over the cream. Make sure it is closed well. Cut off any excess dough. Brush the dough with milk. Bake for 30 minutes. Cool on a cooling rack for 15 minutes. Take out of pan. Let it cool off completely. Sprinkle with cocoa powder.

Chocolate and Cream Pie
Crostata di Crema e Cioccolata

Crust (see short crust I recipe)
Pastry cream (see recipe)
Confectioner's sugar
Cocoa Powder.

Make the pastry cream according to the recipe. Divide the cream half. In one ½ add a ¼ cup of bitter cocoa powder. Mix well with a whisk until the cream is chocolate Set aside the creams. Make crust according to the recipe. Heat oven to 350°. Grease and flour an 8 inch pan. Place the dough into the pan. Pour the chocolate cream into the crust. Level the cream off with a spoon. Pour the remaining cream over the chocolate cream. Cover with the remaining dough. Make sure that it is closed well. Cut off any excess dough. Brush the dough with milk. Bake for 30 minutes. Cool on a cooling rack for 15 minutes. Take out of pan and cool off completely.

FOR DECORATION: Using paper or a cardboard box, cut five 1 inch strips. Set aside. Sprinkle the pie with confectioner's sugar. Slowly place the paper strips over the confectioner's sugar, leaving 1 inch between each strip. Sprinkle cocoa powder over the strips. Slowly take the strips off the cake.

Cream and Apple Pie
Crostata di Mela e Crema

Pastry Cream (see recipe)
Crust (see short crust I recipe)
2 Apples
1 Tbsp. sugar

Make cream according to recipe. Set Aside. Peel and cut 1 ½ apples into ½ inch pieces. Add the to the cream and mix well. Set aside. Make crust according to recipe. Heat Oven to 350°. Grease and flour an 9 inch pan. Place crust into pan. Pour the cream into the crust. Cover the cream with the remaining dough. Make sure that it is closed well. Cut off any excess dough. Brush the dough with milk. Peel and slice thinly the remaining apple. Forming a circle in the middle of the pie, place the slices of apples on the pie. Sprinkle the sugar over the apples. Bake for 30 minutes. Cool for 15 minutes on a cooling rack. Take out of pan and cool off completely. Sprinkle with confectioner's sugar.

Bavarian Cream with Amaretto Cookies
Bavarese con Amaretti

FOR BAVARIAN

Pastry cream (see recipe)
12 oz. heavy cream
2 oz. confectioner's sugar
1 oz. rum
12 gr. gelatin sheets
1 lb. amaretto cookies

FOR SAUCE

12 oz. heavy cream
1 tsp. instant coffee
2 Tbsp. honey

Place the gelatin sheets in cold water for 10 minutes. Prepare the pastry cream according to the recipe. Set aside. Place sugar and 10 ounces of heavy cream in a medium bowl. Whip cream with electric beater until whipped cream is formed. Set aside. Heat 2/3 of the rum for 1 minute. Drain the gelatin sheets and add to the warm rum. Stir until the gelatin sheets are melted. Add the liquor to the pastry cream. Add the whipped cream to the pastry cream, slowly with a fork with vertical movements. Wet the inside of the ring mold with the remaining rum. Add the cream to the ring mold Level the cream off with a spoon. Place in refrigerator for at least 6 hours. For the sauce, place the heavy cream, coffee and honey in a small pan. Warm, on medium heat, for 1 minute but do not boil. Cool sauce completely. Crush half of the amaretto cookies. Set aside. Take the Bavarian cream out of the ring mold. Slice into 12 slices. Get 6 dessert cups. Place a tablespoon of sauce on bottom of each cup. Place 3 amaretto cookies in the sauce. Place a slice of Bavarian cream on top of the cookies; add some crushed cookies and 1 tablespoon of sauce. Repeat this process until the top of the cup is reached. Finish the top off with crushed cookies.

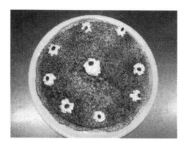

Cappuccino Cake
Torta Cappuccino

3 sponge cake discs
9 oz. mascarpone cheese
2 Tbsp. pancake syrup
4 eggs
1 egg white
4 oz. sugar
2 Tbsp. confectioner's sugar
1 shot espresso coffee
enough espresso coffee to wet sponge cake
Chocolate cream (see recipe)

Make the chocolate cream according to the recipe. Set aside. Separate the three eggs. Place the egg yolks in a small bowl with the sugar and beat on medium speed until they are lemon colored, fluffy and smooth. Set aside. Mix together, in a large bowl, the mascarpone, the syrup and a shot of espresso (if you do not have espresso regular coffee will do). Mix well. Add the mascarpone mixture to the egg yolks. Mix well. Set aside. Add the confectioner's sugar to the egg whites. Beat on maximum speed until stiff peaks are formed. Fold, with a metal spoon, the egg whites into the cream mixture. Mix well. Refrigerate until needed. Using a pastry brush, wet the sponge cake with the espresso coffee. Place the chocolate mixture in between the sponge cake layers. Coat with the mascarpone cream. Sprinkle with ground coffee. Refrigerate for at least 2 hours before serving.

Cream Puffs
Bigné

INGREDIENTS FOR 36 CREAM PUFFS

1 c. water
½ c. butter
¼ tsp. salt
1 c. sifted flour
4 eggs
1 tsp. baking powder

Heat oven to 400°. In large saucepan bring water, butter and salt to a boil. Add flour all at once. Cook on medium heat, stirring constantly until the mixture leaves the sides of the pan and forms a ball. Remove from heat and stir in eggs one at a time. Beating well after each addition. Continue beating until the mixture is smooth and glossy. Add the sifted baking powder and keep beating until well mixed. Using two spoons (or a pastry bag) form 36 small balls on cookie sheets covered with wax paper. Bake for 20 minutes or until the cream puffs are puffed and light brown. (Do not open oven before 20 minutes). Leave to cool completely before filling

Chocolate Covered Cream Puffs Profiterol

Cream Puffs (see recipe)

FOR FILLING

20 oz. heavy cream
4 Tbsp. confectioner's sugar

Place the heavy cream in a large bowl. Add the sugar. Whip on high speed until a stiff peaks are formed. Do not over whip or it will come apart. Place the cream in a pastry bag. Fill the cream puffs from the bottom using the pastry bag tip to make a hole. Set in refrigerator until ready for topping.

FOR TOPPING

6 eggs
6 oz. semi-sweet chocolate
a pinch of salt
10 oz. heavy cream
1 oz. butter
2 Tbsp. confectioner's sugar

Separate the eggs. Set aside. Melt the chocolate with the butter over boiling water. Set aside and let it cool. When the chocolate mixture is cool, add the egg yolks stirring quickly with a wooden spoon. Set aside. Add the salt to the egg whites and beat on high speed until stiff peaks form.

Add, with a wooden spoon, the egg whites to the chocolate mixture and stir well. Set aside.

Place the heavy cream in a medium sized bowl. Add the sugar. Whip on high speed until a stiff cream is formed. Do not over whip or it will come apart. Add, with a wooden spoon, the whipped cream to the chocolate mixture. Make sure the cream is well mixed. Place some chocolate cream on the bottom of an oval platter. Place the cream puffs on top of the chocolate. Place a spoonful of chocolate over the cream puffs. Place more cream puffs on top of the chocolate forming a pyramid. Place a spoonful of chocolate over each cream puff. Continue the process until there are no more cream puffs then pour the remaining chocolate over the whole platter. Refrigerate at least an hour before serving. Any remaining cream puffs can be kept in the refrigerator for 2 days or can be frozen for a later date.

Saint Honor's Cake
St. Honore

CRUST
2/3 c. flour
1 egg
1 Tbsp. sugar
1/3 c. butter, softened e cut into small pieces
A pinch of salt
½ c. cold water

FOR THE FILLING
1 – 9 inch sponge cake disk
1 c. Heavy Cream
2 Tbsp. confectioner's sugar
Pastry cream (see recipe)
Chocolate Cream (see recipe)

CREAM PUFFS
(see recipe), make ½ a batch

FOR CAKE FILLING: Place the confectioner's sugar and heavy cream in a large bowl. Mix on high speed until whipped cream is formed. Place in refrigerator until needed. Prepare pastry and chocolate cream according to recipes. Set aside. **FOR THE CRUST**: place the flour, salt and sugar on a flat, floured surface. Make a hole in the middle. Place the butter and the egg yolk (save the egg white for after) in the hole. Add the water slowly and start kneading the dough until a soft, but not sticky dough is formed. Make a ball. Flatten a little. Cover with a clean, floured dish cloth and place in the refrigerator for at least 30 minutes. **CREAM PUFFS**: Heat oven to 400°. Make according to recipe. Place dough in a pastry bag and set aside. Do not bake. **FOR THE CAKE**: Draw a 9 inch circle on wax paper. Roll out the crust dough to cover the 9 inch circle. Place the wax paper on a cookie sheet. Wet the edges of the dough with the egg white. Distribute the cream puff dough all around the edge of the rolled out dough, to form the edges of the crust. Using a fork, poke holes into the base of the crust. Place in oven and bake for 30 minutes. With the remaining cream puff dough make the cream puffs and bake according to the recipe. Let the crust cool off completely before filling. When the cream puffs are cooled off fill with the pastry cream and set aside. **PUTTING THE CAKE TOGETHER**: Place the remaining pastry cream into the crust. Level off. Place the sponge cake disk on the cream. Brush the sponge cake with milk. Place the chocolate cream over the sponge cake. Place the whipped cream in a pastry bag. Squeeze a line of whipped cream across the top of the sponge cake at 1 inch intervals and all around the cake. Place the filled cream puffs on the whipped cream, around the edge of the cake. Refrigerate for at least 24 hours before use. Sprinkle with confectioner's sugar. Enjoy.

INDEX OF RECIPES

APPETIZERS—ANTIPASTI — 8

Toasted Bread with Tomatoes—Bruschetta	9
Tomatoes and Fresh Mozzarella—Caprese	9
Grilled Vegetables—Verdure alla Griglia	10
Marinated Tuna Fish—Tonno Marinato	11
Steamed Clams—Vongole al Vino Bianco	11
Clams and Mussels in Marinara Sauce—Zuppa di Cozze e Vongole	12
Mussels in White Wine Sauce—Cozze Marinara	13
Mussels in Red Sauce—Cozze Pepate	14
Baked Clams or Mussels—Cozze o Vongole Gratinate	15
Baked Scallops—Capesante Gratinate	16
Clams Casino—Vongole Ripiene	17
Fried Squid or Fried Mixture—Calamari Fritti o Fritto Misto	18
Squid and Artichoke Salad—Insalata di Calamari e Carciofi	19
Octopus Salad—Insalata di Piovra	20
Marinated Octopus—Tagliata di Piovra	21
Seafood Salad—Insalata di Mare	22
Shrimp and Asparagus—Salad Mare e Monti	23
Shrimp and Asparagus—Salad II Mare e Monti II	23
Fried Mozzarella—Mozzarella Fritta	24
Mozzarella in a Carriage—Mozzarella in Carrozza	25
Rolled Eggplants—Involtini di Melanzane	26
Boiled Eggs with Rosé Sauce—Uova con Salsa Rosa	27
Omelet—Frittata	27

SOUPS—ZUPPE — 30

Pasta and Beans—Pasta e Fagioli	31
Vegetable Soup—Minestrone di Verdura	32
Tortellini Soup—Tortellini in Brodo	33

SALADS—INSALATE — 36

Grand Salad—Insalatona	37
Chef's Salad—Insalata dello Chef	38
Chick Pea Salad—Insalata di Ceci	38
Tomato and Red Onion Salad—Insalata Calabrese	39
Summer Salad—Insalata d'estate	39

PASTA DISHES—PRIMA DI PASTA — 42

Pasta Salad—Penne Caprese	43
Pasta Salad II—Penne al Carpaccio	43
Rice Salad—Insalata di Riso	44
Rice with Treviso Salad and Smoked Cheese—Risotto alla Trevisana	45
Tortellini with Ham and Cream—Tortellini Panna e Prosciutto	46
Gnocchi with Eggplant and Mozzarella—Gnocchi alla Sorrentina	46
Gnocchi with Mushrooms and Walnuts—Gnocchi con Funghi e Noci	47
Gnocchi with 4 Cheeses—Gnocchi ai Quattro Formaggi	47
Ravioli with Shrimp—Ravioli dello Chef	48
Tagliatelle with Swordfish and Asparagus—Tagliatelle Spada e Asparagi	48
Tagliatelle with Shrimp and Asparagus—Tagliatelle Gamberi e Asparagi	49
Tagliatelle with Porcini Mushrooms—Tagliatelle ai Porcini	50
Tagliatelle with Sausage and Rucola—Tagliatelle Rustiche	50
Tagliatelle with Filet of Sole and Spinach—Tagliatelle all'Adriatica	51
Fresh Pasta with Monkfish—Pasta Fresca alla Pescatrice	51
Tagliolini with Caviar and Vodka—Tagliolini alla Russa	52
Fettuccini with Salmon in a Cream Sauce—Fettuccini al Salmone	52
Pasta Marinara	53
Pasta with Tomato Sauce—Pasta al Pomodoro	53
Pasta in a Meat Sauce—Pasta al Ragù	54
Pasta in a Vegetable Ragù—Pasta con Ragù di Verdure	55
Pasta in a Pesto Sauce—Pasta al Pesto	56
Linguine with Ricotta—Linguine Simpatia	56
Penne with Tomato and Pesto Sauce—Penne Spadellate	57
Penne with Chicken and Vegetables—Penne Colombiana	58
Penne with Hot Tomato Sauce—Penne All'Arrabbiata	59
Roman Penne—Penne alla Romana	59
Penne with Eggplant and Mozzarella—Penne alla Siciliana	60
Penne with Salmon and Arugola—Penne con Salmone e Rucola	60
Penne in Rosé Sauce—Penne Macrì	61
Penne with Mushrooms—Penne alla Boscaiola	62
Penne with Vegetables—Penne Ortolana	63
Penne with Crab Meat—Penne alla Polpa di Granchio	64
Penne with Shrimp, Crabmeat, Arugola and Mushrooms—Penne Mare e Monti	64
Bows with Zucchini and Saffron—Farfalle Zucchine e Zafferano	65

Bows with Gorgonzola and Arugola—Farfalle Zola e Rucola	65
Mexican Bows—Farfalle alla Messicana	66
Bows with Cherry Tomatoes—Farfalle alla Mediterranea	67
Linguine with Pancetta—Linguine alla Amatriciana	68
Bows with Broccoli in a Rosé Sauce— Farfalle con Broccoli in Salsa Rosa	69
Spaghetti with Squid in a Hot Sauce—Calamari Fra Diavolo	70
Linguine with Spinach and Shrimp—Linguine Fantasia	71
Spaghetti in a White Clam Sauce—Spaghetti alle Vongole	72
Spaghetti in a Red Clam Sauce—Spaghetti alle Vongole–Rosse	73
Linguine with Mussels—Linguine Tarantina	74
Baked Spaghetti with Seafood—Spaghetti al Cartoccio	75
Tagliatelle with Seafood—Tagliatelle allo Scoglio	76
Penne with Shrimp and Zucchini—Penne dello Chef	78
Spaghetti with Olive Oil, and Hot Pepper— Spaghetti Aglio, Olio, e Peperoncino	79
Spaghetti with Clams and Mussels—Spaghetti alla Levantina	80

BEEF DISHES—SECONDI DI MANZO   82

Sliced Beef with Lemon—Carpaccio	83
Beef with Rosemary—Tagliata Rosmarino	84
Beef with Mushrooms—Tagliata con Funghi	85
Beef with Green Peppercorns—Tagliata al Pepe Verde	86
Rolled Beef—Involtini di Manzo	87
Steak with Balsamic Vinegar—Straccetto	88
Steak with Herbs—Bistecca alle Erbe	89
Steak Pizzaiola—Bistecca alla Pizzaiola	90
Steak with Vegetables—Entrecotte alla Contadina	91
Filet Mignon with Porcini Mushrooms—Filetto con Porcini	92
Filet Mignon with Green Peppercorns—Filetto al Pepe Verde	93

VEAL DISHES—SECONDI DI VITELLO   94

Veal in a Tuna Sauce—Vitello Tonnato	95
Veal with Prosciutto and Sage—Saltimbocca alla Romana	96
Veal with Ham and Cheese—Vitello alla Valdostana	97
Veal with Porcini Mushrooms—Scaloppe ai Porcini	98
Veal in a White Wine Sauce—Scaloppe al Vino Bianco	99
Veal in a Lemon Sauce—Scaloppe al Limone	100
Veal and Asparagus—Scaloppe con Asparagi	101
Veal Pasquale—Scaloppe alla Pasquale	102
Veal Macrì—Vitello alla Macrì	103

Veal Sorrento—Scaloppe Sorrentino	104
Veal Chop Cutlet—Cotoletta di Nodino	105
Veal Chops with Cherry Peppers—Nodino All'Agro	106
Veal Steak—Bistecca di Vitello	107
Veal and Peppers—Spezzatino di Vitello	108
Veal Roast—Arrosto di Vitello	109

PORK DISHES—SECONDI DI MAIALE — 110

Pork Chops with Tomatoes and Mozzarella—Braciole con Pomadori e Mozzarella	111
Roast Pork with Milk—Arrosto di Maiale al latte	112
Pork Chops with Apples—Braciole alle Mele	113

CHICKEN DISHES—SECONDI DI POLLO — 114

Chicken Primavera—Pollo Primavera	115
Chicken with Scallions—Pollo con Cipollotti	116
Chicken Marsala—Pollo al Marsala	117
Chicken Pasquale—Pollo alla Pasquale	118
Chicken Macrì—Pollo Macrì	119
The Chef's Chicken—Pollo dello Chef	120
Chicken and Potatoes—Pollo con Patate	121

TURKEY DISHES—SECONDI DI TACCHINO — 122

Turkey in a Butter and Sage Sauce—Tacchino con Burro e Salvia	123
Turkey with Almonds and Walnuts—Tacchino Mandorle e Noci	123
Rolled Turkey—Involtini di Tacchino	124

SEAFOOD DISHES—SECONDI DI PESCE — 125

Mixed Seafood Grilled—Misto Griglia	126
Sea Bass Baked in Salt—Branzino al Sale	127
Grilled Seafood Primavera—Pesce Primavera	127
Sole Fish in a Lemon and Wine Sauce—Sogliola alla Mugnaia	128
Baked Swordfish with Arucola—Tagliata di Spada con Rucola	128
Swordfish with Porcini Mushrooms—Tagliata di Spada ai Porcini	129
White Sicilian Swordfish—Spada Siciliana-In Bianco	130
Swordfish in a Red Sauce—Spada Siciliana	131
Filled Squid—Calamari Ripiene	132
Shrimp Macrì—Gamberoni alla Macrì	133
Shrimp Pasquale—Gamberoni alla Pasquale	134
Monkfish in a Red Sauce—Pescatrice Rossa	135
Monkfish with Saffron—Pescatrice allo Zafferano	135

Salmon with Butter and Sage—Salmone Burro e Salvia	136
Salmon in an Amaretto Sauce—Salmone All'Amaretto	137

VEGETABLE DISHES—SECONDI DI VERDURA 140

Asparagus Parmigian—Asparagi alla Parmigiana	141
Asparagus with Eggs—Asparagi alla Bismarc	141
Eggplant Parmigian—Melanzana alla Parmigiana	142

SIDE DISHES—CONTORNI 143

Escarole and Beans—Scarola e Fagioli	144
Baked Broccoli—Broccoli Gratinati	144
Breaded Fennel—Finocchi Gratinati	145
Sautéed Spinach—Spinaci Saltati	146

DESSERTS—DOLCE 148

Chocolate Salami—Salame di Cioccolata	149
Cooked Cream—Panna Cotta	150
Caramelized Cream—Crème Caramel	151
Pick Me Up—Tiramisù	152
Limoncello Cake—Torta al Limoncello	153
Short Crust Pastry I—Pasta Frolla I	154
Short Crust Pastry II—Pasta Frolla II	154
Pastry Cream—Crema Pasticcera	155
Pine Nut and Cream Cake—Torta della Nonna	156
Fruit Tort—Crostata di Frutta	156
Ricotta Pie—Crostata di Ricotta	157
Chocolate and Pear Pie—Crostata di Pere e Cioccolata	157
Chocolate and Cream Pie—Crostata di Crema e Cioccolata	158
Cream and Apple Pie—Crostata di Mela e Crema	158
Bavarian Cream with Amaretto Cookies—Bavarese con Amaretti	159
Cappuccino Cake—Torta Cappuccino	160
Cream Puffs—Bigné	161
Chocolate Covered Cream Puffs—Profiterol	162
Saint Honor's Cake—St. Honore	163

Printed in the United States
By Bookmasters